ISLANDS OF THE WEST

ISLANDS OF THE WEST

From Baja to Vancouver

Photographs by Frans Lanting
Text by Page Stegner

Sierra Club Books

San Francisco

The Sierra Club, founded in 1892 by John Muir, has devoted itself to the study and protection of the earth's scenic and ecological resources—mountains, wetlands, woodlands, wild shores and rivers, deserts and plains. The publishing program of the Sierra Club offers books to the public as a nonprofit educational service in the hope that they may enlarge the public's understanding of the Club's basic concerns. The point of view expressed in each book, however, does not necessarily represent that of the Club. The Sierra Club has some fifty chapters coast to coast, in Canada, Hawaii, and Alaska. For information about how you may participate in its programs to preserve wilderness and the quality of life, please address inquiries to Sierra Club, 530 Bush Street, San Francisco, CA 94108.

Text copyright © 1985 by Page Stegner.

Photographs copyright © 1985 by Frans Lanting (except where otherwise credited). All rights reserved. No part of this book may be reproduced in any form or by any electronic or mechanical means, including information storage and retrieval systems, without permission in writing from the publisher.

The publisher gratefully acknowledges the cooperation of the following institutions in granting permission to reproduce the historical photographs and illustrations included in this book:

The Bancroft Library, University of California, Berkeley: Pages 7, 24–25, 39, 85, 122

The Santa Barbara Museum of Natural History, Channel Island Archives: Page 50

McNally & Loftin, Publishers, Santa Barbara, California (photograph from *The Legendary King of San Miguel,* by Elizabeth Lester, 1979): Page 48

The British Columbia Provincial Museum, Victoria, B.C.: Pages 110, 112

The Provincial Archives of British Columbia: Pages 4, 88, 89, 120

The engravings reproduced on pages 70 and 74 are from *Harper's Monthly* (1874).

Portions of this book originally appeared in altered form in *Audubon* ("Gem of the San Juans") and *California Magazine* ("The View from Above").

Library of Congress Cataloging in Publication Data
Stegner, Page.
    Islands of the West.

    Bibliography: p.
    Includes index.
    1. Pacific Cost (North America)—Description and
travel.   2. Islands—Pacific Coast (North America).
3. Natural history—Pacific Coast (North America).
I. Lanting, Frans.   II. Title.
F852.3.S74   1985   979   85-2164
ISBN 0-87156-844-6

Frontispiece: Islet in Queen Charlotte Strait, British Columbia.

Jacket and book design by Dana Levy, Perpetua Press
Maps by Earth Surface Graphics
Printed by Dai Nippon Printing Company, Ltd., Tokyo, Japan

10 9 8 7 6 5 4 3 2 1

CONTENTS

He who has never seen himself surrounded
on all sides by the sea can never possess an idea
of the world, and of his relation to it.

Goethe

PREFACE

A BOOK TITLE, because of its brevity, often implies an inclusionary view of the subject it attempts to describe that the material between its covers does not attempt to fulfill. It is perhaps necessary, therefore, to say a few words about what this book is and is not. Neither the text nor the photographs pretend to be more than a sampling of the vast offshore region that lies between the Canadian border and the tip of Baja California. We did not want to write an illustrated sailor's guide to the eastern Pacific, an updated *Coast Pilot* with pictures, nor have we the scientific credentials to undertake a comprehensive natural history of every isle and atoll that pokes its nose above the southeasterly sweep of the California Current. We chose, rather, to focus attention on a single island within a group of islands, and to stress as much as possible our personal involvement with the territory we covered.

The selective approach seemed more suited to our overriding purpose—the expression of our conviction that the islands that sparsely dot our western continental shelf still constitute the most invaluable natural laboratory in our territorial waters for the study of marine mammals, seabirds, and intertidal organisms, and that in spite of the many abuses they have sustained, they have better survived the effects of human intrusion than their counterparts along the Gulf Coast or the Atlantic seaboard. Everything that can be done to protect and preserve them should be done. The continent stretches before us no more.

We pursued our subject sometimes together, sometimes alone, but it was never our intention to directly echo each other's work. The photographer no more wished to illustrate the writer's text than the writer wished to caption the photographer's pictures. It remains our belief that an independent, though cooperative, vision can better express the ambiance of an island environment, the mystery and magic that is sometimes lost in discussions of ecology, geomorphology, and archaeology.

Many people were extraordinarily generous with their time and support in the making of this book. The writer would particularly like to thank Dr. Burney J. LeBoeuf, Dr. Joanne Reiter, Dr. James Estes, Jim Borrowman, Bill Mackay, William Ehorn, Lynn Moultray, the Scripps Oceanographic Institute and the crew of the *Ellen B. Scripps,* the Point Reyes Bird Observatory, the U.S. Fish and Wildlife Service, the National Park Service, and finally Marion, who put up with all the comings and goings and gave her encouragement throughout.

INTRODUCTION

THE VIEW FROM ABOVE

O n the wall in my studio I have a large aerial map of the United States, one of those cartographic inserts that fall out of one's monthly copy of the *National Geographic* like a Cracker Jack prize and get stuffed into a drawer with the Rand McNally road atlas and the official Hotchkiss guide to greater downtown Denver. For some reason I hung this one up. I stare at it whenever the muse decides to be just anybody's girl.

The map is a mosaic of several hundred photographs taken by a Landsat spacecraft from 567 miles above the earth, and it outlines, among other things, the great perplexity of isles, islets, atolls, spits, tongues, necks, capes, harbors, bights, and gunk-holes that characterize our Atlantic seaboard. It outlines, just as dramatically, the virtual hiatus of such configurations along the California, Oregon, and Washington coasts. Except for Puget Sound the satellite image of our western shore is unwrinkled all the way from the mouth of the Columbia River to San Francisco Bay, a distance of 600 miles. There is one small blip just off the Point Reyes peninsula that marks the Farallons, then nothing for another 300 miles south. No Mount Deserts, Cape Cods, Nantuckets, Long Islands, Chesapeake Bays, Pamlico Sounds, Georgia Sea Islands. No shoals, no cays, no keys. For nearly a thousand miles the seasick sailor has limited options when he hunts for shelter out here.

Below Point Conception, above Santa Barbara, where the mainland profile looks as if someone had taken a shallow bite out of California's hind end, Landsat offers some small encouragement. Four grey smudges show up in the Santa Barbara Channel, four more flank the San Pedro Channel and the Gulf of Santa Catalina, three more lie a few miles off Imperial Beach near the Mexican border. In the satellite's eye they look like ships anchored along a dent in the North American plate. From any PSA flight bound for San Diego they look like just what they are, the northernmost in a chain of islands that stretches for 500 miles from Point Eugenia, near Guerrero Negro in Baja, to Point Conception—sixteen bleak and battered protrusions of eroded rock, narrow beaches, low vegetation, wind, fog, and swirling sea mist, varying in size from 134 square miles to as little as one-fifth of a square mile.

The satellite eye says nothing about coastal demographics. If it did, the story of offshore occupation in the East would fill volumes; the western region, with the exception of Puget Sound and the San Juans, might warrant a few pages. Of the eight islands that lie below the Mexican border, only one (Isla Cedros) can really claim habitation. The rest consist largely of sand and beds of tortured riprap transforming themselves into cobble. Of the eight that lie within United States territorial waters, one (Santa Catalina) hosts a small tourist town and a resident population, two (San Clemente and San Nicolas) are property of the Navy, and three (Santa Barbara, Anacapa, and San Miguel) belong to you and me—designated by Congress in 1980 as the newest in our system of national parks. The remaining islands off southern California are private property. Santa Rosa is owned by the Vail and Vickers Corporation, which runs about five thousand head of cattle on it; Santa Cruz is owned jointly by the Stanton and Gherini ranches and the Nature Conservancy. Eventually Santa Rosa and a portion of Santa Cruz are supposed to be included in Channel Islands National Park, though when the transfer from private to public ownership will take place is still unclear.

Off northern California there are only two islands (or island groupings)—tiny Año Nuevo, a few miles north of Monterey Bay, and the Farallons, five granitic rocks of about 111 acres in sum that lie thirty miles due west of San Francisco along the edge of the continental shelf. The former is a State Reserve controlled by the California Department of Parks and Recreation; the latter a National Wildlife Refuge under the jurisdiction of the U.S. Fish and Wildlife Department. Public lands. Which is to say they belong to you and me as well.

You and me will find it somewhat difficult, however, to inspect our property should

Page viii: Surf and reefs at twilight, Año Nuevo Island.

Western gull on nest, Anacapa Island, Channel Islands.

Aerial view of the Santa Rosa Island coastline, Channel Islands.

the spirit move us. For one thing navigation around all of California's offshore real estate (with the exception of Santa Catalina—connected to the mainland by a ferry service) can be hazardous under certain conditions. Weather can change in a matter of minutes. Blue sky and a mild breeze can be suddenly transformed into dense fog and gale-force winds; a flat sea unruffled as a millpond can turn into five- and six-foot swells; Capt'n Bligh can be enjoying his preprandial noggin on the poop deck one minute and sailing on his ear the next. It requires one's attention.

For another thing anchorages and landing sites are few and at best involve a white-water adventure through rolling surf. Visitors to Santa Barbara Island ride in with the surge and leap off their rocking boats onto a metal ladder. Similar acrobatics are required at the eastern end of Anacapa. On the Farallons one is plucked from one's ship by a shore-based crane and swung up, clinging to a sort of trellis of twine attached to a truck tire, onto a pierlike affair. At Año Nuevo there *is* no access except by rubber boat across a reef beset by winds that break on one's hapless dinghy from both sides. Harbor seals body-surf alongside, waiting for the real show to begin. One can get ashore at all these places, to be sure, but it takes effort and skill, and is not without risk. Most folks are content to keep their topsiders dry and stay out in the swells.

But the major impediment to visitation—suggesting that fifteen years of developing environmental consciousness has finally gotten at least limited translation into official policy—is officialdom as represented by the National Park Service, Fish and Wildlife, the Nature Conservancy, the Point Reyes Bird Observatory, Vail and Vickers, Dr. Carey Stanton; in short, all those organizations and individuals charged with the stewardship of California's islands and their diverse wildlife populations. In various degrees all do their best to protect the native flora and fauna from the earnest sightseer who clomps around the fragile environment mashing plant life, pestering birds and marine mammals, pock-eting a few "artifacts" from Indian middens, and occasionally falling off a cliff. Activities are therefore restricted. On the Farallons only biological and ornithological researchers are generally allowed; only a few educational and scientific excursions are permitted on Santa Cruz and Santa Rosa; user-days are limited on the National Park islands and visitors' movements are severely circumscribed. Protection of seals and sea lions, bird life, endemic plants, and archeological sites is given top priority by the islands' custodians, and it's a good thing too. The public track record, even in this awkward environment, hasn't been all that hot.

The successive native cultures that inhabited many of the southern islands for at least 7,000 (possibly 30,000 to 40,000) years before the arrival of the white man managed to live in reasonable harmony with their waterbound world. They had neither the numbers (about two thousand by the time Spanish missionaries relocated them to the mainland and engaged their services in the fields of the Lord) nor the technology to foul it up. But

Bunchberries, Pacific Rim National Park, Vancouver Island.

by the end of the eighteenth century commercial hunting of the enormous colonies of seals, sea lions, and sea otters began, and over the next hundred years succeeded in virtually eliminating pinnipeds (fin-footed marine mammals) from the California coast—indeed, from the entire southern biogeographic region of the eastern Pacific. By the time an International Fur Seal Treaty was signed in 1911, only a few remnant groups were left to save.

While the sealers were denuding the beaches of marine mammals, sheep ranchers went to work on the inland flora. Through overstocking and overgrazing they gradually reduced both pasture and woodland to desert. Through the introduction of cats, rats, rabbits, goats, and pigs, they set in motion changes in endemic biotic communities that would never be reversed. In no sense of the word were these islands ever *populated* by European man, but it took only one lightkeeper with a couple of pet Belgian hares, or one shepherd with a taste for goat's milk, to start unravelling millions of years of natural selection. Perhaps the only islands between Baja California and the Pacific Northwest *not* to have suffered from overgrazing and the introduction of exotics are the Farallons—and they were barren to begin with. They did not escape, however, exploitation by pre-Sierra Club man, whose 1850s representatives developed a lip-smacking fondness for murre eggs. Between the founding of the Farallon Egg Company in 1855 and the turn of the century an estimated fourteen million omelets were gathered on South Farallon (a serious impaction on the breeding colony, one assumes), and the continuous presence of rapacious hominids on these rocks had a devastating effect not only on murres but other bird life as well. In order to reduce competition from scavenging gulls (which also had a taste for embryonic murre) gatherers routinely stepped on gull eggs and chicks as they went about their business.

Post-Sierra Club man doesn't go around traipsing on occupied nests. We have learned that when we are excessively greedy and take all the eggs in the basket, allow for standing room only in the pasture, or destroy one part of an ecosystem to promote growth in another, we are the ultimate losers. But we have not yet learned (or are unable to learn) to adapt our habits to our habitat; we are not actually convinced that our collective presence in the wilderness is disruptive; and we are certainly unwilling to consider the proposition that there are places on earth where we might not need to go at all. So the restraints that have been imposed by governmental agencies and private individuals controlling public access to most of California's islands are probably the only way to insure an acceptable recovery from the sins of our past.

From the California border to the tip of Washington's Olympic Peninsula, the smooth line of the Landsat coast is broken only by the mouth of the Columbia, Willapa Bay, and Grays Harbor. No islands whatsoever. Then, as if to make up for unconscionable neglect, business picks up with a vengeance—the San Juans, the Canadian Gulf Islands, Vancouver Island, that whole broken littoral through the Strait of Georgia, Johnstone Strait, Queen Charlotte Sound, Hecate Strait. Somewhere in some musty file numerical statistics for this vast archipelago must exist, but the merest sample indicates how utterly unalike this part of the Pacific is from its southern counterpart. At high tide the San Juans alone number over 450 "islands," some of them no more than cairns poking above the water, others encompassing a land area over fifty square miles. There are another two hundred in British Columbia's Gulf Islands just to the north, along the leeward side of Vancouver Island (itself over 13,000 square miles in size), and hundreds more as one follows the Inside Passage north to Port Hardy and Cape Scott.

Much of this entire region remains pristine wilderness, though much of it is being ferociously logged, overfished, and loved to death by ever increasing hordes of tourists. It harbors the world's largest concentrations of orcas, or killer whales. Bald eagles are so

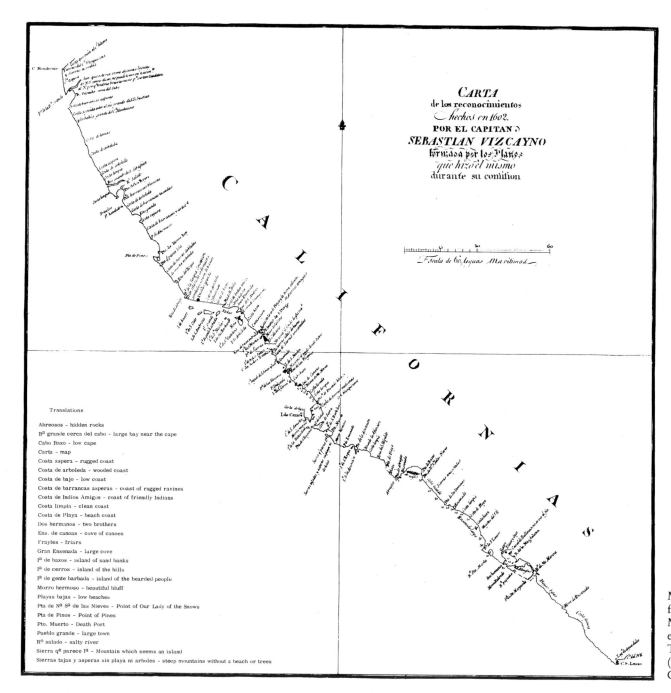

Translations

Abreosos – hidden rocks

Bª grande cerca del cabo – large bay near the cape

Cabo Baxo – low cape

Carta – map

Costa aspera – rugged coast

Costa de arboleda – wooded coast

Costa de bajo – low coast

Costa de barrancas asperas – coast of rugged ravines

Costa de Indios Amigos – coast of friendly Indians

Costa limpia – clean coast

Costa de Playa – beach coast

Dos hermanos – two brothers

Ens. de canoas – cove of canoes

Frayles – friars

Gran Ensenada – large cove

Iª de baxos – island of sand banks

Iª de cerros – island of the hills

Iª de gente barbada – island of the bearded people

Morro hermoso – beautiful bluff

Playas bajas – low beaches

Pta de Nª Sª de las Nieves – Point of Our Lady of the Snows

Pta de Pinos – Point of Pines

Pto. Muerto – Death Port

Pueblo grande – large town

Rº salado – salty river

Sierra qᵉ parece Iª – Mountain which seems an island

Sierras tajas y asperas sin playa ni arboles – steep mountains without a beach or trees

Map of the Baja and California coast from Cabo San Lucas to Cape Mendocino, from the 1602 expedition of Sebastian Vizcaíno. The Channel Islands and Cedros ("Cerros") can be identified. Courtesy Bancroft Library.

Young elephant seal, Año Nuevo Island.

commonplace one grows blasé and forgets to notice. Chinook and coho salmon run in such quantity that any piscator with a hoochie and a hook can snag *something* for dinner. Oysters crowd the shore; there are shrimp in the northern inlets. Cedar, hemlock, and Douglas fir cover the mountainous terrain in growths so thick that clearcutting is the only method that allows them to fall (or so the argument goes). In short, the area is incredibly rich in natural resources, and because of its climate (it is referred to locally as "the banana belt" and the "Mediterranean of the Pacific") and its abundant rainfall, it seems limitless in its ability to provide. It isn't, but it is going to be some time before that message is broadly heard.

Environmental problems in the Northwest, when they arise, are concerned with questions of multiple use far more than is the case on islands in the southern biogeographical region. They have to be. There are 7,000 permanent residents on the Canadian Gulf Islands, 350,000 on Vancouver Island, and 8,000 on the San Juans. It is a little unpopular to talk about limits and restrictions in the face of such a population, many of whom are hell-bent to turn the place into a field-and-stream paradise for sportsmen, tourists, retirees, second-homeowners, and urban in-migrants; many others of whom are hell-bent to turn it into board-feet and pulp products. Ninety percent of Vancouver Island, for example, is forested, and ninety percent of the forests are leased to lumber companies. One-third of the total work force is employed in the lumber business. As for the tourist business, one old joke goes that B.C. stands for Brochure Country and not, as rumor previously had it, British Columbia.

Not everywhere in the San Juans is a Friday Harbor, of course, and not all of Vancouver Island is Victoria. The Nature Conservancy owns and manages several preserves in the San Juans, the U.S. Fish and Wildlife Service has designated some minor islands and rocks as bird and marine-mammal refuges, the Canadian and provincial governments have established a few parks. Many of the islands are uninhabited (so far), and there are the usual citizen groups who doggedly fight the lumber industry, the fishing industry, the speculators and developers. But timber and tourism constitute the region's economic base, and as long as there is a buck to be made off what appear to be endlessly bountiful natural resources, "environmental protection" is not soon going to gain ascendancy in the collective Northwest conscience.

Preservation remains, however, the major concern on the more fragile island environments off the California coast. Aided by such legislation as the Marine Mammal Protection Act and the Coastal Zone Management Act, recovery in some areas is not only a hope but is actually taking place. The possibility of a total relapse in the aftermath of a massive oil spill remains a threat, but southern sea otters, once thought extinct, have returned to an estimated population of 1,600 to 1,800 animals—though none have yet recolonized any of their island habitats. Guadalupe fur seals, which were not even resighted until 1928, are approaching 2,000 in number—though again no breeding colonies have returned to the California islands, and only a few males have been sighted off San Miguel and San Nicolas. Not yet a cause for celebration, perhaps, but better than extinction. The northern fur seals, whose only breeding ground in the eastern Pacific south of the Pribilof Islands is on San Miguel, numbered 100 individuals in 1968. Today that tally has increased to over 2,000. And there are now thought to be stable communities of harbor seals and California sea lions throughout the Channel Islands as well as farther north at Año Nuevo and the Farallons. The elephant seal has become . . . ubiquitous. Virtually extinct by 1915, the world population now totals over 50,000 animals.

Unfortunately, the fascination man has with viewing wild creatures in their native habitats is not reciprocated. Only the elephant seal seems somewhat indifferent to the presence of man in his midst. All other pinnipeds are panicked by an incautious approach; their sudden exodus into the water resembles a stampede and occasionally results in the crushing or abandonment of newborn pups. Sufficiently disturbed, seals and sea lions have been known to abandon breeding areas altogether. So have seabirds. A 1980 environmental assessment of the Channel Islands by the National Park Service observes in reference to three species of cormorants that nest there: "All . . . are known to be extremely sensitive to human disturbance. A single, appropriately timed disturbance can result in a total reproductive failure when a colony is flushed by a single intensive event." I suppose even a greenhouse slug might eventually take umbrage at repeated intrusion. For that matter, human beings might suffer reproductive failure if every time they headed for the harem they encountered a boatload of tourists.

So it seems not unreasonable to argue that, in the few places presently unsullied by human development, we preserve them as they are, and that, moreover, we leave their biotic communities to their own devices—not merely unmolested but unobserved. As in *alone*. It is a paradox, to be sure—federal land, public land, much of it (in the words of the Park Service mandate) set aside "for the benefit and enjoyment of the people." And yet the most sensible assessment of that benefit is to keep the people down, if not out, and to protect the brown pelican, the island night lizard, and the globose dune beetle from the island sightseer and the peregrine snoop.

We will not, of course, leave these regions unobserved. The coastal islands that dot our Pacific shore are generally regarded as far more important than mere refuges for marine mammals and seabirds; they are, from north to south, isolated preserves for environmental studies of all kinds. Where they have not been destroyed by abuse or the occasional natural disaster, they are (*because of* their isolation) invaluable laboratories for close scrutiny in

Gilford Island, British Columbia,
from the air.

Brown pelican hovering over surf.

fields from paleoethnology to paleontology, from biogeography to biogenetics. It was, indeed, precisely because of the species isolation unique to islands that Darwin was able to support his theory of evolution by natural selection with such a rich body of evidence. And I suppose it might be argued that if we hadn't given him a permit to clatter around on the Galapagos we might still be confident that the earth was created in six days.

The controlled environment that many of the islands of the eastern Pacific provide enables us to study not only the phylogenetic development (survival and extinction) of rare biotic communities, but much about our own origins as well. As Don Kelley, the first editor of *Pacific Discovery,* put it, an island is like a theater in the round: ". . . an observer can not only watch every entrance and exit but can see the direction of each actor's coming or going." We must, no doubt, go and observe. But we might, as we do so, keep Aldo Leopold's warning in mind: "To cherish we must see and fondle, and when enough have seen and fondled, there is no wilderness left to cherish."

ON THE WATERFRONT

ISLA CEDROS, BAJA

The Western Flyer *hunched into the great
waves toward Cedros Island, the wind blew
off the tops of the whitecaps, and the big guy
wire, from bow to mast, took up its vibration
like the low pipe on a tremendous organ. It
sang its deep note into the wind.*

John Steinbeck
The Log from the Sea of Cortez

About halfway down the Baja Peninsula, that long finger of the North American Desert that separates the Gulf of California from the Pacific Ocean, the land curves west-northwest like a cup hook to form in its hemicycle Bahia de Sebastián Vizcaíno and Scammon's Lagoon, famous birthing and breeding ground of the California grey whale. Fourteen miles off the tip of the hook at Punta Eugenia lies the largest of Mexico's west coast islands, Cedros, famous for nothing and righteously ignored by the Automobile Club of Southern California in its travel guide to tropical hot spots south of the border. Which is a pity. It seems to me the perfect spot to consign all those drivers of RV caravans that now form a continuous, unbroken queue from Tijuana to Cabo San Lucas, who clearly need a break on the way down. Leave the old bus in Guerrero Negro and take the champagne flight over the bay. Have dinner at La Pacelita, Cedros's finest. If the auto club wants to consider this suggestion and include the island in its list of tourist facilities, recreational opportunities, and points of interest, I'll be happy to write the copy.

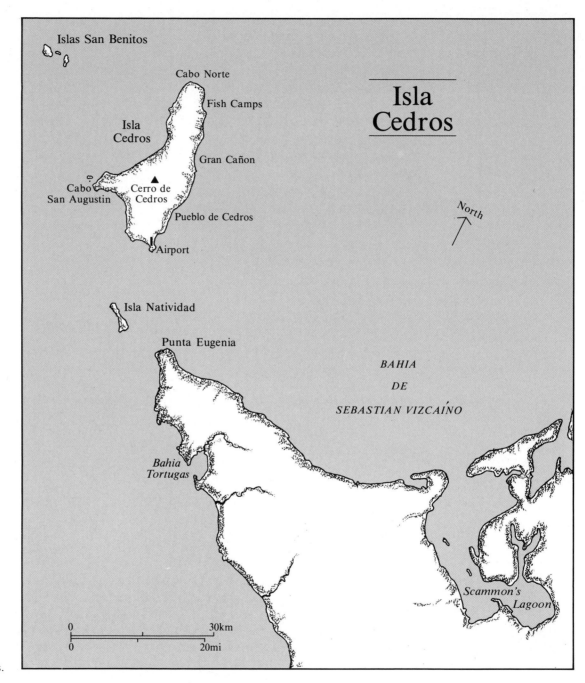

Islas San Benitos

Cabo Norte

Fish Camps

Isla
Cedros

Gran Cañon

▲

Cabo
San Augustin

Cerro de
Cedros

Pueblo de Cedros

Airport

Isla Natividad

Punta Eugenia

BAHIA

DE

SEBASTIAN VIZCAÍNO

*Bahia
Tortugas*

North

Isla
Cedros

*Scammon's
Lagoon*

0   30km

0   20mi

Page 14: Winter storm, Cabo Norte, Cedros.

Route Description: Reachable by plane or private yacht. Rejected C-47 from the Tarzana Air Circus may leave Guerrero Negro Tuesdays, Thursdays, Saturdays. Also it may not.

Accommodations: Casa de Huespedes Aguilar. Open all year. Single $4. Double $4. Ménage à trois $4. Spacious cubicles, some with bed-type arrangements for sleeping. No phones. No TV. No air conditioning. No bath. Also no *bebidas alcoholicas* or *drogas* allowed in rooms.

Language: Spanglish spoken at one *tienda* on the main street. Otherwise the American tourist need not concern himself. Gringos are sullenly ignored by the locals.

Health Conditions and Services: Unspeakable.

General Comments: Advisable when visiting Cedros to bring your own breakfast, lunch, and dinner. Also carry U.S. currency to bribe the mayor. He regrets that you have no permit for your camera, your eyeglasses, your pocket knife, your wooden leg, but he will, for $20, overlook his obligation to deport you.

The smudged window of the plane and the low altitude from which we are approaching the southern point of the island make it impossible to get more than a fleeting impression of Cedros, but a fleeting impression is enough. It looks like a pile of rusted scrap, dun-colored, arid, barren, a heap of broken rubble, a wasteland, sulphurous, infernal. To the less hysterical it merely looks like what it is, an extension of the Sierra Vizcaíno of the mainland, stranded by a submergence that began nearly 100 million years ago (in the late Mesozoic Era) of that once continuous mountain range. Geologically speaking it is composed of metamorphic rocks—serpentines, schists, sandstones, cherts—with considerable granitic intrusions at its northern end and evidence of volcanic action during the Tertiary Period at its southwestern corner. Not very much is definitively known about its age, but the strata laid upon its core appear to go back at least 135 million years. It sports three eroded peaks over 3,000 feet (the highest, Cerro de Cedros, rising to nearly 4,000), 134 square miles of faulted, twisted, upheaved slates and shales, and along its southeastern shore a town so depressed and squalid that even Hieronymus Bosch couldn't have imagined it.

On the other hand, Cedros has been a kind of sanctuary for seafaring folk ever since the sixteenth century, a place to take on wood, replenish water supplies, and hunt down a goat or two to augment a diet of hardtack and salt pork. Pirates found its southern bight a convenient spot in which to lie in wait for galleons laden with silver. It was an invaluable port for both whalers and sealers during the nineteenth century. And there is some ecological evidence that it roughly marks a dividing line between northern and southern species of a number of marine fauna found along the Baja Peninsula. However dreary in appearance, it is not without significance.

At the airport a single taxi serves all who need a ride to the village or the salt docks on Cabo San Augustín. I notice that the price of admission (extracted in advance) is unabashedly higher for the gringo than for the latino, but I feel no inclination to argue about it. The driver's general demeanor suggests he'd forego a fee for the pleasure of watching me walk the four miles into town, and I get the distinct impression that my Anglo hide isn't all that respected out here in the sand barrens. Maybe it's my cleft-palate Spanish.

The salt dock, however, is a stunner. In order to drop one of my fellow travellers at the company compound, we drive west toward Pico Redondo and eventually come to an astonishing mountain of sodium chloride, a hundred feet high, it seems, a block wide, a mile long. Well . . . perhaps not quite, but from my cramped perspective in the back of the taxi it looks like a crystal cordillera. It also employs a good many people on the island and expands an economic base previously dependent on fishing.

Salt has been produced in natural flats around Scammon's Lagoon on the mainland since the late 1850s, and in major quantities since 1957 when a company called Expatadora de Sal began exploiting this natural resource in earnest. A 50,000-ton annual quota escalated to 3 million tons between 1957 and 1967, most of it hauled off in supertankers for consumption in Japan and the United States. Cedros became useful in the process because supertankers can't navigate very well in shallow lagoons and evaporation ponds. Flat-bottomed barges are loaded at Guerrero Negro and carry the salt (3,000 tons a day) out to the island, where a deep-water port enables it to be loaded on the bigger ships.

My driver just shrugs when I ask him how big these stockpiles actually are. Perhaps the arteries around his heart have been hardened by their proximity. But he is more loquacious in responding to my query as to a suitable hotel in which to stay. *"No hay hotel,"* he says. Well, all right, if *no hay* hotel, where do people stay? *"Cuartos."* Does he know of any, then? This time his shrug involves a slight tilt of the head that could mean anything but at least indicates more than the absence of information. I sit back in my seat and peer at the hills of yellow shale. This is out of my hands.

By the side of the road a goat browses thoughtfully on what appears to be a discarded spool of telephone cable, indifferent to the hurtling taxi and the cyclone of dust that engulfs it. Over a rise a few shacks appear, their gaudy colors startling against the faded tones of the earth around them, and then suddenly we are around a corner and descending into the village in a clutter of dogs, kids, chickens, and general midmorning foot traffic. No noticeable change in our velocity. At the end of this broad, unpaved street (the main drag), and just before I think we are about to launch off the quay into the harbor, my amigo hangs a left up an alley just wide enough for his clattering Chevy and lurches to a stop in front of a two-story structure still in the mid-stages of construction—or abandoned after the siding was installed. The Aguilar Guest House. Casa de Huespedes Aguilar. *Para un día o una vida.*

Islas San Benitos at dawn.

Later, after a slash of nerve tonic I sneak in defiance of the enunciate nailed to the wall outside my cell—*"Quede extrictamente prohibido ingerir bebidas alcoholicas y toda clase de drogas en los cuartos"*—I walk down to the beach that fronts the town and out along the breakwater that forms the harbor. Above the blue corrugated metal of the fish cannery buildings (the island's only economic enterprise other than salt), the twin towers of a church rise against a barren hillside terraced by the paths of human and animal. A few palms grow in scattered clumps between the disarray of ramshackle houses, pastel shanties in aquamarine, purple, orange, fuchsia, and behind this all, rising in a series of softly eroded ridges to a rust-colored peak, Cerro de Cedros, or Cedar Hill. It is perhaps in keeping with the town's image that it calls its 3,950-foot mountain, "hill," and the smattering of juniper woodland at its top, "cedar." The beach itself is black with oil, cluttered with abandoned machinery, and redolent with the corpses of a half-dozen rotting pinnipeds washed up above the tide line. Dead from natural causes, perhaps, or from potshots taken by local pescaderos. *No sé.* In the broad valley that fans upward behind the center of town, the rusted hulks of automobiles and trucks lie scattered like upturned beetles, and the slope fairly glitters in the refracted brilliance of a million busted bottles.

Productos Pesqueros, the cannery, is a cooperative owned by the island's fishermen, many of whom live for extended periods in a shanty camp on the northern end. Originally built in 1920 by a German firm in order to process abalone (a nontaxable export once its natural shell was replaced by tin), the Mexicans took it over in 1935 and gradually, as the abalone beds were diminished, introduced other seafood to their canning line. Cedros is extraordinarily rich in a variety of fish and shellfish—the Pacific sardine, Pacific yellowfin tuna, California bluefin tuna, bonito, Pacific mackeral, and spiny lobster *(Panulirus interruptus),* flown live from the island to Ensenada and thence to markets in the United States. Nearly a quarter of Baja's lobster catch comes from these waters.

The area is also rich in California grey whales. Twice a year the greys, migrating to and from the lagoons at the end of Bahia Sebastián Vizcaíno, Laguna San Ignacio, and Bahia Magdalena use Cedros as a navigation point, swimming in more or less a straight line from Punta Baja, a hundred miles to the north, and either turning east into Laguna Ojo de Liebre when they reach the island or rounding Punta Eugenia and continuing south. The absolute predictability of the California greys' migration to their birth place in late December and January added significantly to the near extirpation of the species when their major Baja breeding grounds were discovered by Captain Melville Scammon near the middle of the last century.

Captain Scammon had been whaling during the summer and fall of 1857 in and

Agave and elephant tree, Cedros.

around Bahia Magdalena. Business was bad, and rather than return to San Francisco with his oil casks empty, he persuaded his crew to remain at sea longer than they had bargained for to help him look for a great lagoon reported by the Indians to lie somewhere to his north—a lagoon, the stories went, full of whales. Scammon anchored his bark, the *Boston,* in deep water somewhere between Cedros and Punta Eugenia, and sent a small tender schooner along the lee shore of Bahia Vizcaíno to search for a possible opening that would mean an inland waterway in the Vizcaíno desert. Unfortunately for the whales, the schooner succeeded in discovering a navigable passage into the breeding grounds; the *Boston* followed, and a familiar scene unfolded.

It took Scammon only eight months to fill out his cargo (indeed, everything that would hold oil was employed as a cask for the trip home)—eight months to accomplish what normally took four years. It took those who learned of his discovery only a few subsequent years to reduce the population of greys to a level that was no longer profitable to hunt. Since most of the whales killed in the lagoon were females with their calves (newly born or unborn) the long-term effect on the breeding population was extraordinary. Even Scammon himself, in his classic study *The Marine Mammals of the Northwestern Coast of North America*, wondered "whether this mammal will not be numbered among the extinct species of the Pacific."

The International Whaling Convention, signed by seventeen nations after World War Two, prohibited the taking of grey whales, and over the years the California herd has slowly recovered. From near extinction at the turn of the century, they now number around 15,000 animals, but it is anybody's guess how the increased popularity of "whale watching," and boat traffic in general in Scammon's Lagoon and Bahia Magdalena, may affect migration and reproduction. So far the whales seem amiably indifferent.

Walking along the path out toward the end of the jetty I try to ignore the assault on my senses from the decomposing seals floating in the greasy water by the cannery and the general aura of dilapidation emanating from the village behind it. Not exactly the ambiance that greeted Francisco de Ulloa on the 20th of January, 1540, when he stepped out of his dinghy and proclaimed this paradise the property of the King of Castile. The Ignacieño Indians who were living here at the time didn't think so, but they were mistaken. They were too few, too poorly armed with rocks and sticks and "little bows with which they could hardly have killed sparrows," and in any event Ulloa really only cared about replenishing his ship's supply of wood and water before sailing on. It wasn't worth dying for, although at least several Indians did. "Our Lord was pleased," Ulloa observed, "that when we had shot a few of them we landed. . . ."

But Cedros was hardly a plum to Spanish adventurers with their eyes glazed by fantasy and their dreams fixed on Cíbola, those seven fabulous cities in New Mexico reputed to contain unimaginable wealth—in fact, nothing more than a handful of squalid

Child's grave, Cedros.

Children with kites, Pueblo de Cedros.

Morning light on Cedros hills.

View of the Island de Cerros on

Zuni pueblos. The record indicates only one other distinguished visitor, Sebastián Vizcaíno, who stopped by in 1602 on his way to discover Monterey Bay and who, like Ulloa, reported the aboriginal inhabitants in possession of "implacable dispositions." Compelling an attitude adjustment seemed not to be Vizcaíno's style, and after taking on wood and water he continued north in search of the elusive Strait of Anian (the rumored northwest passage).

The implacable disposition of Cedros islanders was not, unfortunately, implacable enough. In 1732 a Jesuit priest named Padre Taraval journeyed to Huamalgua (Fog Island, as the natives called it) from his mission at San Ignacio, 150 miles to the southeast. Theopathy in his heart, he somehow managed to convince the heathens that he could save their souls if they would give up running around naked, adorning themselves with white paint, poking holes in their ears for trinkets, idling away their time spearing fish and sea turtles, and would come with him to the mainland. He took them to Mission San Ignacio, where they were shortly treated to a smallpox epidemic and all died. An old story, oft repeated as the "black robes" moved north.

east of California, The Peak N 46 E°. dist off shore 5 or 6 Leag°.　　　*John Sykes*

Watercolor profile of the "Island de Cerros" from
Captain George Vancouver's expedition, drawn
approximately 1793. Courtesy Bancroft Library.

Before dinner (though I have yet to see anyplace that looks remotely like a cafe, and
my appetite hasn't impelled me to ask) I walk back behind the town through the junked
cars and the acres of nonbiodegradable disposables—the cans, bottles, plastics, old tires,
refrigerators, bedsprings—and climb the sedimentary hills that ascend to the foot of
Cerro de Cedros. The principal vegetation is a sparse growth of desert scrub and a weird
tree called a *copalquin* that seems to want to grow parallel to the ground instead of up
toward the sky. Actually it is the perpetual wind through here that dictates its angle of
repose. Also known as the elephant tree *(Pachycormus discolor)* because of its grey color
and its resemblance to an elephant's trunk, the *copalquin* is one of the most common
species of vegetation on the eastern side of the island, along with agave and a dense bush
sunflower.

At higher elevations and along the northern ridges of the mountains there are a few
juniper woodland areas (the "cedars" for which Cedros is misnamed) and some pine
forests (mainly bishop pine). But the alpine fantasy conjured up by these floral types is
quickly dispelled by the other major generic classifications found on the island—chaparral,

Fishing village, Islas San Benitos.

maritime dune scrub, coastal sage scrub, desert scrub. There is no botanical designation for the ubiquitous paper scrub, easily identified by its festoon of white blossoms used in the arrangement of the napkin nosegay and the Kleenex corsage. It is, regrettably, everywhere in evidence as I return to the village in search of something to eat.

La Pacelita. It is a public house, I assume, by the *cumbia* blasting out of the blown speaker of a jukebox. Inside are a short bar and a half-dozen tables that seem likely to collapse under the weight of an elbow. Most of the tables are occupied by cannery workers, each with a quart bottle of beer in his fist. There is no chatter going on, no laughing, no conversation, no Miller-time conviviality, just sullen drinking and the tap-tap-tap of a cigarette in an ashtray. These guys could have been brought in by George Grosz to model for one of his grim little proletarian satires.

I take a seat at the one empty table and timidly order a beer. Don't want to get out of step, might not leave here alive. Before I notice that nobody else is eating I ask the waitress if there is food. *"Sí,"* she says, *"menudo."* And then, perhaps interpreting my glum look as indifference to tripe (particularly as I have made its acquaintance on the

Opuntia cacti, Cedros.

plane from Guerrero Negro, along with its satellite flies), she remembers. *"Hay camarones."* Camarones it is, then.

And they are excellent little shrimp, plump, juicy, served in a peppery broth with a pile of tortillas and beans on the side. Since I am the only pink person in the place (for that matter, on the island), as well as the only one eating, I am a bit unstrung and eat without relish. I am not much gratified to observe out of the corner of my eye that a particularly swarthy young turk who has been staring at me since I came in is now rising from his chair, beer and cigarettes in hand, and heading across the room toward my table. This is it. A few insults. Then he's going to cut my gizzard out with his switchblade.

"Americano?" he says, settling himself down.

I hang my head. It's not my fault. I'm not responsible for immigration laws, territorial fishing restrictions, the death of the *bracero* program, the battle of Resaca de la Palma, the Bear Flag Revolt.

"So am I," he says in English, slapping me on the shoulder. "I lived in Ontario. You know Ontario?"

"Canada?"

"No, man, Ontario, California. L.A. Where you live?"

"Santa Cruz. It's near San Francisco."

"Santa Cruz." He considers this thoughtfully for a moment, then lights up. "I know Santa Cruz, man, it's where that big tree is with all the roots. I kiss that tree whenever I go by. Biggest tree in the world, man, *en todo el mundo.*"

"I think you're thinking of that banyan tree in Santa Barbara," I say.

"Santa Barbara. Yeah, maybe Santa Barbara, I forgot. . . ."

Ramón, as he says he is called, has a habit of drifting off into pensive reflection, as if politeness demands cogitation. In between reveries he tells me, with a sweeping gesture, that everybody in the room is crazy, that *he* is crazy, that he lives on Cedros to avoid U.S. authorities who want to put him in prison, that he would like another beer, that he has a *panga* (boat) and will take me to the north end of the island to show me the seals. I tell him, in turn, that I don't think he is crazy, not at all, that I would be privileged to buy him another beer, and that I would love to go see the seals but I unfortunately only have one more day before returning to the mainland.

"No problema, man," he says. "We can go *mañana.*"

I do not expect to see Ramón again, but he shows up at the Aguilar at six-thirty in the morning and shouts *"Hola, gringo!"* until I stumble out of my room. His *panga* is one of those open, fiberglassed affairs endemic to the west coast of Mexico, about eighteen feet long, V-hulled, with a fifty-horse Evinrude clamped on its transom. Accompanied by an entourage of western gulls we pick our way through the flotsam in the harbor and turn north, following the rocky coast toward Cabo Norte and the small fishing village

Blooming agave, Cabo Norte, Cedros.

just to the southeast of the point. There are flocks of black brants in the water, a coastal goose that summers in Alaska and winters around Cedros, the Benitos, and the Baja lagoons, and a great number of brown pelicans that flap sedately up and down, keeping a weather eye cocked for breakfast.

The steepness of the island as it lifts out of the sea is reminiscent of the Big Sur region in north central California, though not as dramatic. The cliffs are sheer, rising one to 200 feet before the gradient of the mountains eases the ascent, and broken in only a few places by precipitous lateral canyons that yawn into alluvial fans of cobblestone and broad sandy beaches. We slow and circle off the major break (called Gran Cañon—what else?), and look up its sclerotic gorge to the very spine of Cedros itself, the transverse ridges that span the length of the island from north to south. Ramón says that *scientíficos* come to this section of the coast to look for a rare kind of seal, he doesn't remember what.

"The Guadalupe fur seal," I tell him.

"The Guadalupe fur seal," he says, as if from the reverb might issue enlightenment.

During the early 1800s sea otters, elephant seals, and the Guadalupe fur seal were thick on Cedros, as they were throughout the islands of Baja and as far north as Point Conception above Santa Barbara. By the end of the 1800s the fur seal was thought to be extinct, wiped out by Russian, Aleut, and American sealers who harvested them by the hundreds of thousands—130,000 in two years on Guadalupe, according to one report, though another claims it took twenty-five years for depletion. The good ship *Eliza* out of New York recorded 38,000 skins in one season on the Juan Fernandez Islands off Chile; the *Betsy* 100,000 for her year in the same region. It hardly matters if the reports are exaggerated. By 1895 the Guadalupe fur seal was gone.

Except . . . not quite. In 1926 two fishermen, one appropriately named Harry Fisher, the other William Clover, sighted a few animals again on Guadalupe and reported the news to Dr. Harry Wegeforth of the San Diego Zoological Society. Wegeforth commissioned Clover to capture a pair for the San Diego Zoo, then decided for some reason not to pay Clover's bill when the mission was accomplished. Clover said fine, he'd retaliate by going back to the island and killing the few seals that still remained. It was a threat he evidently failed to carry out successfully, because there is now a resurgent colony of over one thousand fur seals on Guadalupe. The two animals on display at the zoo, however, died in less than a year—at about the same time that poetic justice caught up with their captor and snuffed him out in a barroom brawl in Panama.

There has been no scientifically demonstrated repopulation of Cedros, though a few animals have occasionally been seen just north of Gran Cañon and may gradually be returning. Ramón and I don't see any, however. All we see is a pair of raucous ravens arguing over some tidbit below them on the rocks. Farther north at least a dozen osprey

Western gulls, Cedros.

California sea lion in surf, Cedros.

Sand dollar, Cedros.

Downtown Cedros.

nests hang from the ledges and buttresses of the cliffs, and their tenants are soaring just offshore over our heads, their high-pitched cry audible even over the idling motor. Unlike other hawks the osprey feeds entirely on fish, hovering over its prey and then crashing into the water talons first, but either these guys have had brunch or our presence disturbs them. They float up over the cliffs on the thermals, flap vigorously a time or two, and glide along the slope of the mountain, lost against its conforming colors.

We stop for an hour at the fishing camp at Cabo Norte, ten or twelve shacks occupied mainly by young bachelors who often stay out here for several months at a time. Most are out plying their trade, joined no doubt by a trailing herd of thieving sea lions whose rookeries are located on both sides of the point and partway down the western side. The few men we meet are considerably friendlier than their counterparts back in town, though they seem a little disappointed that I have not come bearing copies of *Hustler* and *Oui* to trade for lobster. They will have to wait to catch up on their reading for the whale-

Elephant tree in evening light, Cedros.

Tour boats anchored off Islas San Benitos.

watching tours that stop on their way to the lagoons. Ramón drops off several cartons of canned goods and agrees to carry back a sizable crate of rockfish; we shove the *panga* off the beach and begin the three-hour journey back. "Tonight I take you to the whore house," Ramón says, starting the engine.

"To the whorehouse . . ." I intone.

I do not go to the whorehouse. Moral, ethical, and hygienic reasons deflect interest. I need no communicable memories of this decaying village. Instead I go to bed before it is even dark and lie in my sweltering, windowless cubicle wondering if my amigo the taxi driver, who promised for an advance payment of 500 pesos to take me to the airport in the morning, will, in fact, show up.

There is no problem with the taxi driver. He shows up right on time. The question is whether the plane from Guerrero Negro will show up, and if it does, whether it will have the incentive to depart. There seem to be a number of variables, most of them listlessly discussed by the small crowd assembled on the tarmack at the end of the runway—*if there is enough cargo to justify a flight, if there are enough passengers, if the motors work, if the* piloto *is sober, if'n the weather be good.* The sun swarms up over the fog that blankets Bahia Vizcaíno and glares hotly on the yellow hills. Eventually I hear the distant drone of engines somewhere beyond the point, and after an anxious interval see the silver glint of wings in the refracted light. Salvation. There is much on this blasted pile of rock to fascinate a naturalist, no doubt, and I would be the first to recommend it. But even God took his Sundays off.

AMERICAN GALAPAGOS

THE CHANNEL ISLANDS

*It has been said that we have mastered the art
of taking everything apart. In the Channel
Islands it is possible for man to begin to
understand the science of putting it all back
together. The land stretches before him no more.*

Barry Holstun Lopez

For nearly an hour I've been watching our approach to the northern Channel Islands on the radar scope, a cup of coffee gimballed in one hand, a brass rail clenched in the other. The *Ellen B. Scripps,* a 90-foot, steel-hulled research vessel from the Scripps Oceanographic Institute in San Diego, plows through the winter swell, smashing her blunt nose into the wind-driven sea like a pugnacious whale. Heavy spray lashes the bridge, runs aft across the fantail and out through the open transom. In the predawn darkness, safety seems to depend largely on the green sweep of that radar beam with its ghostly reconstruction of coast, offshore drilling rigs, shipping traffic, and the treacherous islands that dominate the Santa Barbara Channel. Even when daybreak begins slowly to penetrate the storm cover, the demarcation between ocean and sky is indecipherable.

We are on our way up from San Clemente and San Nicolas, headed for San Miguel, the westernmost island in this chain of submerged mountaintops off the southern California mainland. Pleistocene topography, the geologists tell us. I read learned papers on

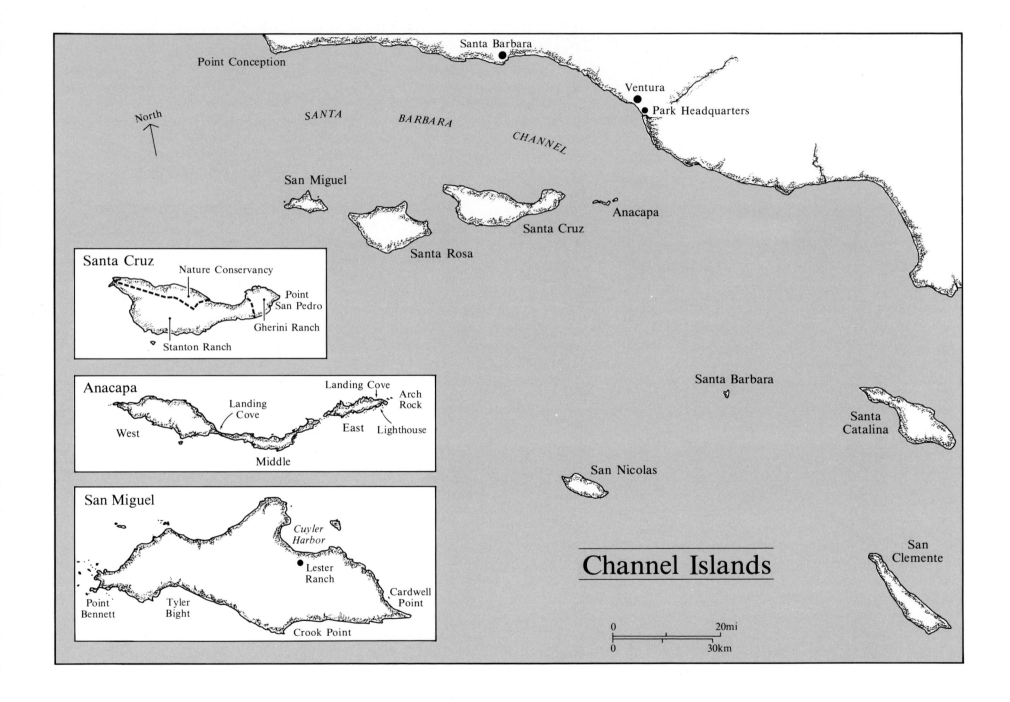

North

Point Conception

Santa Barbara

Ventura

Park Headquarters

SANTA *BARBARA* *CHANNEL*

San Miguel

Anacapa

Santa Cruz

Santa Rosa

Santa Cruz

Nature Conservancy

Point San Pedro

Gherini Ranch

Stanton Ranch

Anacapa

Landing Cove

Landing Cove

Arch Rock

West

East

Lighthouse

Middle

San Miguel

Cuyler Harbor

Lester Ranch

Cardwell Point

Point Bennett

Tyler Bight

Crook Point

Santa Barbara

Santa Catalina

San Nicolas

San Clemente

Channel Islands

0   20mi

0   30km

Page 36: Sea lions, sleeping elephant seals, and blackbellied plovers, San Miguel.

Scientists on an outing to the Channel Islands in 1889. Courtesy Bancroft Library.

the influence of eustatic oscillation of the sea level on submarine terracing, differential uplift of crustal blocks, tectonic deformation, basin deposition, but the information is too solemn and makes no pictures. What one sees from deck level, and at a distance, is low, faintly blue with haze, and often hard to distinguish from a bank of fog. Up close there is greater topographic differentiation—narrow beach or rocky shelf leading to tawny cliffs, sandfalls from the windswept mesa above, a handful of battered trees emerging from the thin fog like a photographic image in the darkroom tray. Cormorants pose on the jagged dorsal fin of a submerged reef. Sea lions poke curious heads above the rhythmic swells beyond the break. Submergent extensions of California's Transverse and Peninsular Ranges these mountaintop islands may well be, but geomorphology excludes their mystery.

The primary purpose for this expedition has been the continuation of a long-term study of subtidal habitat around San Nicolas in order to assess its suitability as a translocation site for sea otters. That work has been completed with ship time to spare, and University of California biologist Burney LeBoeuf wants to look in on the elephant seal colony at Point Bennett, where he conducted extensive pinniped research back in 1968. The crew doesn't object to this little cruise. The fishing is fabulous off San Miguel.

In the galley we ignore the *Ellen B.*'s simulation of a rodeo bronc and wolf down bacon and eggs and flapjacks and the remnants of last night's cherry cheesecake. Sea legs intact. Nobody hanging his head in the scuppers. By the third cup of coffee the steady drone of the engines subsides, and our floating diner stops pitching and begins to roll in a cross swell. The first mate pauses on his way up to the bridge and remarks that we are in the passage between Santa Rosa and San Miguel, slowing because of the changing topographic configuration of the sea floor (we don't want to run aground) and the poor visibility (we don't want to run on the beach). The weather, he says, seems to be lifting.

Up on deck we have a clear view off the starboard bow at the northeastern flank of San Miguel and Cuyler Harbor, a putative sanctuary protected on the west by Harris Point and on the south by the island itself, but otherwise completely exposed. We have a trailing sea almost directly out of the north, and if we are to have any chance of landing at all we will have to round Cardwell Point and head for Tyler Bight on the southwestern shore. The swells should be blocked by Point Bennett, making a run through the surf in the Zodiac less hazardous—though, as the reef extending out from Cardwell Point seems to testify, less hazardous is a relative term around San Miguel. Breakers converge on the submerged rocks from the north *and* the south—big rolling combers approaching head-on at about 10 knots, meeting in a geyser of whitewater that bursts thirty feet in the air and issues a booming report we can hear from almost a mile away. Because of the winds and the conflicting direction of the cold-water California current and a warm-water countercurrent, the area around San Miguel is said to be the roughest on the Pacific coast.

The electronic equipment available to the captain of the *Ellen B.* as he runs past Crook Point toward Tyler Bight is a far cry from the taffrail log and compass provided the first European to discover the southern California coast in 1542, Juan Rodrigues Cabrillo. Cabrillo, a Portuguese explorer employed by Viceroy Mendoza (Cortes's successor in the Aztec city of Tenochtitlan), journeyed up the coast of California in search of the mythical Straits of Anian and made the first sightings of San Diego Bay, San Pedro Bay, Santa Monica Bay, Catalina and San Miguel islands, Point Conception, and finally "'La Baya de los Pinos"—Monterey Bay. He is generally depicted in artists' sketches sailing majestically along in a large, sturdy Spanish galleon, flags flying and armor gleaming; but the evidence suggests that his two ships, the *San Salvador* and *La Victoria,* were in fact leaky little affairs, at least one of which was built by unskilled natives in Natividad on the west coast of Mexico, and neither of which was equipped with radar, sonar, Loran position finder, CB, VHF, EPIRB, or cherry cheesecake.

East, Middle, and West Anacapa.

Young brown pelican begging for food.

Cabrillo's luck ran out somewhere out there off our starboard beam—his nemesis not a mishap at sea, as befits an explorer in the land of gold and griffins, but gangrene. Walking around on San Miguel he fell and broke his arm. Two months later he died. There is a low monument at Cuyler Harbor, erected in 1937 by the Cabrillo Civic Clubs of California to commemorate the assumption that his bones indeed lie somewhere in the bleak strata of the island, but his grave has never been actually located.

The real discoverers of the northern Channel Islands, it should be noted, antedate Sr. Cabrillo by more than a few years. How many more years, and precisely who the first prehistoric people to live in the region were, are still matters of some speculation and controversy. The clear evidence, from radiocarbon dating of cemeteries on Santa Cruz, Santa Rosa, and San Miguel islands, indicates human occupation as far back as 7,500 years, and more or less continual inhabitation from that time until the early nineteenth century, when the Chumash-speaking Cañalino finally succumbed to imported diseases, the Hispanic penchant for relocating heathens and working them to death, and the toll extracted by Aleut seal hunters, who apparently liked to harvest a few Indians along with their annual quota of pinnipeds and sea otters. Population estimates based on ethnohistorical information from the early mission period in California (1780 to 1790) indicate close to 2,000 individuals living on all of the northern islands except Anacapa. By 1812 they were gone—dead, or assimilated into mission life on the mainland.

The not-so-clear evidence of prehistoric habitation in this area, however, is a good deal more interesting. American anthropology places the earliest appearance of man on this continent at anywhere from 13,000 to 15,000 years ago. Scholars argue, but this is the officially accepted line. In 1975 John Woolley, a geologist working for the Vail and Vickers Corporation on Santa Rosa, discovered a large fire pit three meters in diameter under a thick overburden exposed by erosion. The pit contained both dwarf mammoth bones and primitive stone tools made from a black metamorphic rock not indigenous to the alluvium beds surrounding the pit—in short, imported. Charcoal collected for dating when the site was excavated in April of 1976 showed no measurable radiocarbon activity. It showed itself, in other words, to be *older* than the upper limit of radiocarbon dating, older than *40,000* years.

Skeptics argue that it is only coincidence that the tools and bones and charcoal found at the site all happened to get into the same place at the same time. There are no teeth marks on the mammoth short-ribs to prove the presence of hungry hominids. But the Woolley discovery seems to corroborate what anthropological and archeological researchers such as Philip Orr (from the Santa Barbara Museum) and Rainer Berger (from UCLA) have been arguing for some years—that the evidence of early man in North America, specifically the "barbecue pits" of Santa Rosa, predates official estimates by at least 15,000 to 25,000 years. Orr, who by 1956 had uncovered 160 prehistoric village sites on that one

Sleeping sanderlings.

island, and Berger, who spent more than fifteen years exploring the anthropological record, seem to agree that *conclusive* evidence of a connection between man and mammoth remains elusive.

Tyler Bight is a small chomp out of the southwestern side of San Miguel, protected on the north and to some extent on the west. But the storm that has been battering us all the way down the coast has taken a miraculous break, pulled back to sea and left the entire Santa Barbara Channel in surprised sunshine, and while the long-range weather forecast isn't encouraging, we can sneak in on low tide, spend a few hours at Point Bennett, and still get back to the ship before it starts to blow. Twenty thousand marine mammals lying snout to schnoz on a stretch of beach only a few hundred yards wide and a half-mile long seems to me a sight worth taking a few risks to see.

All of the Channel Islands host colonies of pinnipeds, but San Miguel claims the most diverse population anywhere in the world: six species, including the only breeding colony of northern fur seals south of the Pribilofs, and the increasing presence (though nonbreeding) of the rare and endangered Guadalupe fur seal. Commercial hunting of these animals (as well as harbor seals, Steller's sea lions, California sea lions, northern elephant seals, and sea otters) began at the end of the eighteenth century, and in a hundred years succeeded in virtually wiping out pinnipeds from the southern part of the eastern Pacific. The International Fur Seal Treaty, signed by the United States, England, Russia, and Japan in 1911, was almost too late. Fewer than fifty northern elephant seals remained, a handful of otters, and not enough Guadalupe and northern fur seals to even count. Otter pelts became so rare they fetched $1,700 at their peak. Steller's sea lion was harvested, among other things, for its whiskers. They made nice pipe cleaners. And seal meat in general made excellent cat food for Anglo-European pets.

Thanks largely to the 1911 treaty, and the 1972 Marine Mammal Protection Act, the current news is not as bleak. Southern sea otters have returned to an estimated population of 1,500 to 1,800 animals (as opposed to 120,000 northern sea otters); Guadalupe fur seals, thought extinct until 1928, now number almost 2,000; the northern elephant seal has come back like the termite and the fruit-fly. Burney LeBoeuf recalls that when he began work on San Miguel in 1968 there were approximately 11,000 animals in the breeding colony; today that number has nearly doubled. Farther north at Año Nuevo there were 500 animals in 1968; today there are 3,000.

On the beach at Tyler Bight we change from wetsuits to pants and boots. Behind us the slope rises an abrupt 400 feet, rocky and sandy, held precariously together by a variety

Tree sunflowers on islet off Santa Cruz.

of low-growing plants and prickly pear cactus. At the top it flattens suddenly into a broad mesa, eight miles long and four miles wide. This barren plateau distinguishes San Miguel from the more heavily vegetated mountain/valley configuration of Santa Rosa and Santa Cruz, and from the lush, narrow pitch of middle and west Anacapa. Indeed, Anacapa in the spring, when the coreopsis, paintbrush, goldenfield, and sea-fig are all in bloom, resembles some fantasy by Disney. Santa Barbara, Santa Cruz, and Santa Rosa all turn out in similar display when the weather warms, but San Miguel shows the effects of harder times. Its most startling display of flora is a caliche forest in the center of the island—calcium carbonate root castings, some of them formed more than 14,000 years ago when sand dunes buried existing vegetation and the organic acids in the plants reacted chemically to cement the particles together. While Santa Cruz and Santa Rosa support stands of pine and oak (including one of only two stands of Torrey pine in the world), San Miguel can offer only a ghost forest of concrete snags.

The National Park Service suggests in its general management plan for the region that San Miguel is recovering from previous overgrazing by sheep (prehistoric elephants were the first offenders), but they would have a hard time proving it from the barren look of things at this end of the island. All of the northern Channel Islands have suffered from a variety of introduced creatures—goats, pigs, rabbits, cats, rats, cattle—but sheep are particularly destructive. In sufficient numbers, they will destroy everything when drought renders forage thin, and they have wreaked havoc on the native plants and grasses throughout the eastern Pacific. San Miguel's destruction began in 1863 when a Santa Barbara resident named George Nidever purchased the island and stocked it with 6,000 sheep, 125 cows, and 25 horses. A three-year dry cycle immediately wiped out 80 percent of his animals, but not before they partially denuded the plateau on which they grazed. In varying degrees the same kind of destruction has taken place on Santa Cruz, San Nicolas, Santa Rosa, San Clemente, east Anacapa—indeed, anywhere sheep and goats have been allowed to proliferate. And in some places, like parts of Santa Cruz, the problem has been exacerbated by feral pigs rooting up the fragile soil. Whole hillsides there look as if somebody with a rototiller had run up and down them.

From the mesa above Tyler Bight it is only a mile across the sand and rocks to the bluffs above Point Bennett. The wind rustles the sparse scrub and cools the perspiration as we pause for a moment to catch our breath. Due north, Castle Rock pokes out of the ocean a few hundred yards offshore, and to the east the plateau tilts gently toward Cuyler Harbor and the remnants of the Lester Ranch—another unfortunate sheep operation that stripped the island of much of the greenery it had left. Herbert Lester, a World War One shell-shock victim, made his home here for nearly fourteen years before blowing his brains out, apparently despondent over the news that the Navy intended to use San Miguel as a radar bombing target.

Bloodstained bull elephant seals
in territorial battle.

The only accurate description is barren. Buff-colored rocks, dunes, deep arroyos cut
here and there by erosion, crumbling ledges of sedimentary deposits exposed by wind
and rain. An island fox, not much bigger than a house cat, watches us for a few minutes
from a low hill, then slips quietly into a ravine. An endemic subspecies related to the
mainland grey fox, it is found on all of the Channel Islands except Anacapa and Santa
Barbara, and here on San Miguel in numbers that range in estimate from 151 to 498.

Like much of the California desert that this tableland resembles, appreciation takes a
patient eye and a liking for landscapes that, on the face of it, say nothing—or rather say
only space, silence. There is, of course, "white noise," nondirectional sounds of surf and
wind in the brush, but it is sound that merely sets off the astonishing primordial stillness,

Herbert Lester, the "King of San Miguel," and his family around their distress flag. Courtesy McNally & Loftin, Publishers.

the emptiness that surrounds. Storm-battered though it may often be, there is nothing here today but a great unpronounced attendance—Pleistocene man gnawing the charred bones of his mammoth, Cabrillo transfigured in his grave, Herbert Lester trudging disconsolately to a distant sand spit with his rifle in his hand. Mute ghosts, voiceless time.

At Point Bennett the information is entirely different. Although the peak of the breeding season has passed and many of the females have gone back to sea, the beach is littered with what one might take to be fat, black rocks, if there weren't 15,000 of them and if they weren't moving occasionally to flip sand in their neighbors' faces—and if the heads of harem weren't periodically rearing their scarred, parasite-encrusted, 6,000-pound bulks into the air to warn off some rubber-lipped deviate who has been skulking around the fringe of the sultan's sandbox with cuckoldry on his mind. One of the unfortunate consequences of being born a male elephant seal is that unless you are in the top 5 percent of your class, you are destined to a life of celibacy. While this is not exactly a scientific observation, it is true that a few dominant bulls take care of most of the breeding chores, and there is nothing quite so comic as a hapless young male with a bad case of satyriasis trying to sneak a nooner before he gets his nose bloodied by the mikado.

And some nose it is, too. About two feet long and as big around as a man's thigh. Not exactly an object you'd want to put in your mouth, though that is what the male elephant seal does when he needs a resonating chamber to amplify his opinions—generally at night when he is down at the bottom of some rock-walled cove and the scientific party is up on top in its tent trying to sleep. The tune is revolting, a combination belch and gag, only in the case of the elephant seal the belch is cosmic and the gag sounds like the Colossus of Rhodes choking on a ham.

Breeding season lasts from the time the females head ashore in mid-December to drop their pups until they leave in mid-March to feed for six weeks and regain the enormous weight lost in the period after they give birth. Small wonder. The newly born weigh about 85 pounds when they emerge, but in the three months it takes them to transform from pups to weaners they gain more than 200 pounds, all on Mom's milk. And during this time Mom eats nothing. In fact, she seems to spend most of her time trying to avoid repeated brutalization at the flippers of some three-ton libido.

There are a considerable number of sea lions mixed in with the lethargic elephant seals. More wary of man, they scuttle like a retreating army into the sea at our approach and then bark at us in righteous indignation from beyond the breakers until we move down the beach. A flock of sanderlings skitter along the tide line, poking their sharp beaks into the damp sand in search of amphipods. The islands host a number of seabird breeding populations—storm-petrels, cormorants, auklets, western gulls, guillemots, murrelets, brown pelicans—and if I were a dedicated birdwatcher I could add these sanderlings to the snowy plover, black-bellied plover, oystercatcher, and California gulls

Arch Rock at dusk, Anacapa.

Cowboys and cattle on Santa Cruz Island, 1869. Courtesy Santa Barbara Museum of Natural History.

I have seen today. Not to mention the tangled sticks of a long-abandoned eagle eyrie above Tyler Bight that has somehow managed to survive many seasons of winter storms. Humans drove out the last nesting eagles from the Channel Islands years ago, shooting them for alleged interference with sheep production, or simply for sport from passing boats.

Humans also nearly wiped out the brown pelican by overuse of agricultural pesticides as far north as the Salinas Valley. DDT concentrations in the fish on which pelicans feed affected the shell hardness of their eggs, and it was suddenly discovered in 1970 that reproduction was down to zero. The ban on DDT has resulted in a resurgence of the west Anacapa rookery, the northernmost breeding colony in the eastern Pacific and the only one in U.S. territorial waters. According to Frank Gress, a biologist from the University of California at Davis and an authority on the brown pelican, about 1,500 nests have been counted this year, but the near decimation of the Channel Island population is a clear reminder of the interconnection of ecosystems and the potential hazards of technological tinkering. Spray for leaf-miners in the San Joaquin Valley; kill a pelican on Anacapa.

Dark banks of storm clouds have moved closer to the mainland. I collect a handful of fossil land-snail shells, each about the size of a pea, from one of the many windrows between the dunes while Burney calls the *Ellen B.* on the walkie-talkie to tell the crew we'll be back at Tyler Bight in an hour. They have been standing offshore just outside Adams Cove fishing for rock cod (commonly mislabeled red snapper in most California restaurants) and are not overly pleased to be interrupted. One 55-gallon garbage can full of vermilion, garibaldi, yellowtail, and calico bass isn't enough.

Climbing up the slope from Point Bennett we stop to rummage through an ancient kitchen midden full of broken shells of intertidal organisms (abalone featured prominently), a few caliche-encrusted bones, some simple scraping tools of chipped stone. A sign nearby advises visitors to confine their observations of marine mammals to the bluffs above the point, and indeed the Park Service requires all but research scientists to be accompanied on San Miguel by a ranger. Back on top of the mesa and looking toward the mainland, the whole eastward sweep of the island dissolves in an aura of sea mist thrown up by surf pounding the coast. From the cliffs above Tyler Bight the *Ellen B.* looks like a toy boat rocking in the swells, the Zodiac hauled up on the beach like a frail craft with which to assault the rising swells. We are about to get wet.

B etween San Pedro Point, at the eastern tip of Santa Cruz, and the Ventura mainland we turn south and head toward San Diego. It might be possible to run into

National Park superintendent William Ehorn with pelican chick, Anacapa Island.

the lee of Santa Cruz and see whether the storm will blow itself out during the night, but the marine weather report is so uncompromisingly foul that there seems little purpose served by pitching and rolling for twelve hours just to confirm what is already known. High winds and high seas will make landing anywhere a virtual impossibility, and navigation in the small boat extremely dangerous. Not so secure in the big boat either, as the half-submerged wreck of a freighter off the southern shore of Santa Rosa seems to testify. The submarine terraces around the Channel Islands hold more than a few rusting relics of misdirected shipping.

Anacapa approaches on our starboard bow. The light is burning on its eastern promontory just above Arch Rock, an offshore volcanic slab worn through the center by millions of pounding waves, and we pass close enough so that I can see movement around the old Coast Guard station, now used as a ranger's residence and a visitor center by the Park Service. Water-storage facilities are housed on the hillside above in what appears to be a church—a ruse concocted to discourage boaters who in the past have amused themselves by taking potshots at the tank as they cruised by.

Although facilities are minimal on Anacapa, its proximity to the mainland makes it the most visited of the islands, and its ecosystems the most vulnerable to human intrusion. The Park Service is concerned about the impact of sightseers in the intertidal zone and is studying ways to alleviate the stress that visitation inevitably creates in a fragile habitat. West Anacapa, the domain of the endangered brown pelican, is closed to the public except for the tidepool regions. Middle and east Anacapa have small systems of trails that overlook a number of coves and marine mammal haul-out areas, and that can be similarly closed during critical parts of the year. Ultimately, the acquisition of the east end of Santa Cruz and all of Santa Rosa by the Department of the Interior, and the development of visitor sites on those large islands, should take some of the pressure off Anacapa.

The energy and the authority behind much of the recent concern for preservation of biologic, anthropologic, and geologic resources on the islands belong to William Ehorn, Superintendent of the 250,000-acre national park.* When discussions of changing their status from monument to park first began, a number of people were concerned that inclusion in the National Park System would have little effect in protecting the environments; that, indeed, in any area set aside "for the enjoyment of the public" the possibility of protecting fragile biotic communities becomes extremely difficult, and as a result their value as a place for scientific study is severely limited. But Ehorn has thus far been able to extend the concept of national park well beyond its too often unfortunate manifestation as national resort, and he seems to regard his job, at least in part, as that of custodian

* An area that includes one mile offshore of each of the five islands. A 600,000-acre Marine Sanctuary extends the protected boundaries another five miles offshore, bringing the total area under federal ownership to 850,000 acres.

Sea-fig blossom, Anacapa.

The Stanton ranch, Santa Cruz, from the air.

Researchers tagging a young
elephant seal, San Miguel Island.

of a national scientific and educational preserve. The latter idea was suggested years ago
by Dr. Charles Remington in an article in *Discovery,* a publication of the Peabody Museum of Natural History, and it is one we could well afford to give more attention in a
world of shrinking possibilities. Many of us would be quite content to know we own a
piece of a place where elephant seals and brown pelicans are doing quite nicely, thank
you; no attention need be paid. A kind of National Wildlife Monastery. No visitors.

The Channel Islands National Park, quite obviously, does not exclude visitors. They
are welcome in any number at the park headquarters in Ventura; they are welcome in
numbers limited by permit and under the supervision of a ranger even on remote San
Miguel. But Superintendent Ehorn isn't going to make it too easy or too comfortable. It
will take the kind of effort that discourages people whose idea of a nature walk is from
the RV to a concessionaire cafeteria and back.

In many respects the islands are a kind of success story in a long, dismal history of
environmental abuse, albeit a success story still *in medias res.* What man was once bent on
exploiting to the hilt, and nearly destroyed in the process, he is now trying to restore—

removing, insofar as he is able, the destructive elements he introduced, protecting by law that which he once saw only as fur coats and pipe cleaners, restricting his movements through a wilderness where he acknowledges himself a guest, fighting his own unenlightened kind over the issues of oil drilling and development and mindless vandalism. Quiet in the Monastery. Pinnipeds at prayer.

If officialdom continues to resist pressure to reinterpret "benefit and enjoyment of the people" as comfort, amusement, and entertainment of the people; if the eventual inclusion of Santa Rosa and part of Santa Cruz into the park system doesn't lead to a great network of trails, vista points, nature walks, and campgrounds; if the number of tour companies licensed to ferry people out from the mainland isn't increased from its current number of one; and if all those concessionaire types who think a wilderness experience constitutes eighteen holes before lunch—if they can all be kept at bay, then there is hope that our offshore environment in this particular area will not only survive, but survive in a manner somewhat approaching its original condition.

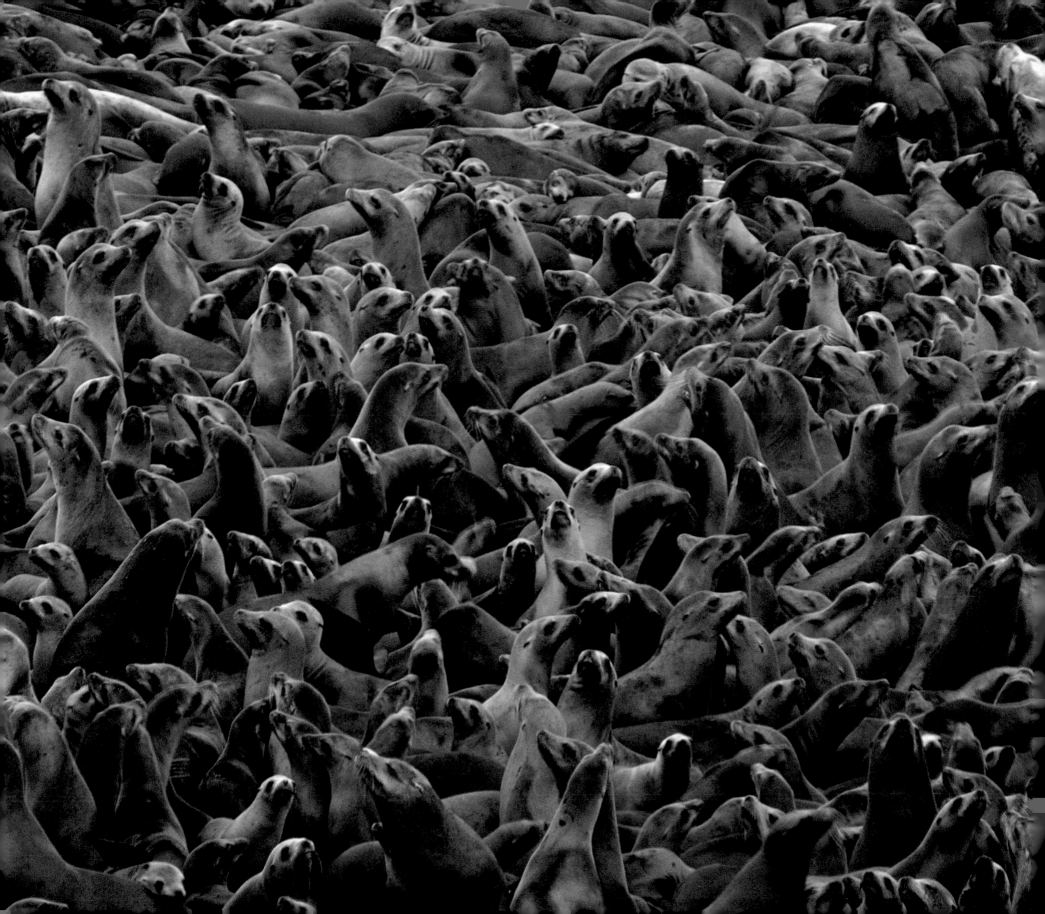

FERTILE ROCKS

AÑO NUEVO AND THE FARALLONS

*We pause in the rush of unloading to stare in awe
at two strapping monsters battling near the water
scarcely 15 yards away. Butting heads, bellowing
threats, feinting and pushing, slashing and tearing
tough blubber neck with canine fangs. Their
ridiculous nasal appendages somehow swinging
clear before each blow. One giant retreats slowly,
bloodying the water in his path.*

Dr. Burney J. LeBoeuf

The moon is in its last quarter, and the path between the old foghorn building and the blockhouse is treacherously faint. If I list too far to starboard it's a precipitous, one-bounce drop into the narrow cove where an irritating subadult elephant seal is practicing phonics by depositing his nose in his mouth and trumpeting at his tonsils; list too far to port and it's into the hole of a defunct catchment basin that once replenished the lightkeeper's bath at this stately mansion on the southeast end of the island. The stately mansion is now a rotting *pension* for sea lions, who took it over when the last resident human left Año Nuevo in 1948.

Calls of nature cannot be indefinitely postponed, however, and the blockhouse— formerly a Coast Guard gasoline storage facility, currently a one-room shelter for researchers studying the island's fauna—has no powder room. Hasn't much else in the way of amenities either—three bunks, a table, a desk, a propane-powered refrigerator and stove. But it is built of cement bricks nearly a foot thick and offers a fortress not only against

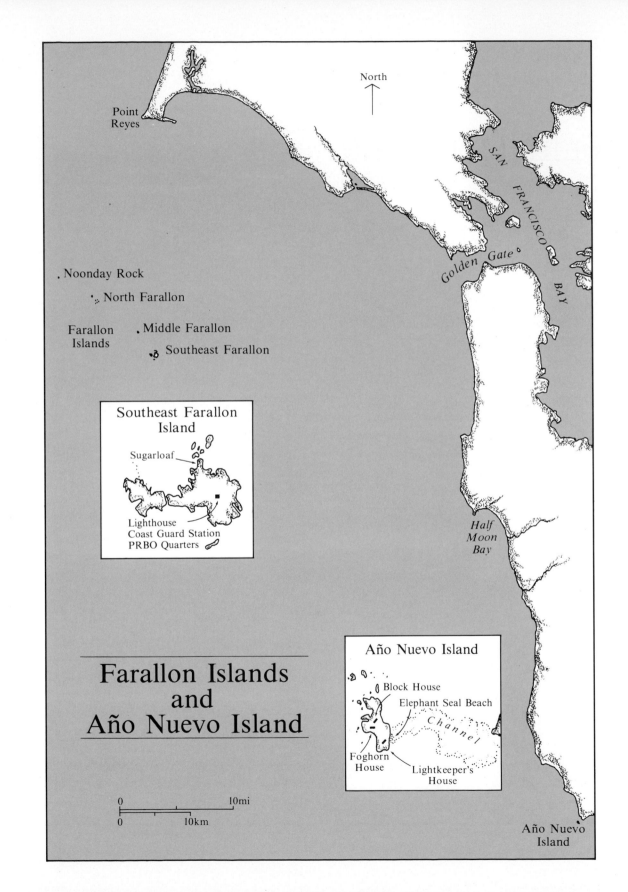

North

Point
Reyes

SAN FRANCISCO BAY

Golden Gate

. Noonday Rock

. North Farallon

Farallon
Islands

. Middle Farallon

. Southeast Farallon

**Southeast Farallon
Island**

Sugarloaf

Lighthouse
Coast Guard Station
PRBO Quarters

*Half
Moon
Bay*

Farallon Islands
and
Año Nuevo Island

Año Nuevo Island

Block House

Elephant Seal Beach

Channel

Foghorn
House

Lightkeeper's
House

Page 56: California sea lions, Año Nuevo.

0   10mi

0   10km

Año Nuevo
Island

the winter rains that sweep in from the Pacific to batter this detached scrap of coastal headland, but from the extreme winds that blast its profile as well. The light shining from its open door and the occasional whiff of steaming mussels that reach me as I totter toward the lee of the foghorn building make it seem almost homey on this windy night.

Twenty miles north of Monterey Bay, fifty miles south of San Francisco, and lying a scant 600 meters offshore, Año Nuevo only recently qualifies as an island at all. Indeed, early accounts describe it as a point rather than an entity detached from the mainland. Although Juan Cabrillo and Sir Francis Drake passed it in 1542 and 1578, respectively, it was not recorded in any ship's log until Sebastián Vizcaíno sailed north from Monterey Bay toward Cape Mendocino in 1602. Father Antonio de la Ascensión, Vizcaíno's chaplain and diarist, named the projection of land they saw Punto de Año Nuevo, but made no mention of an island. Father Crespi, travelling with Gaspar de Portolá in 1769—an overland journey that led to the discovery of San Francisco Bay—referred to the "point of Año Nuevo, which is low with rocky reefs." Still no mention of an island. Captain George Vancouver, surveying this area during his 1792–94 exploration of the northern Pacific, observed that "near Point Año Nuevo [there are] some small rocks detached from the coast a very little distance." But "small rocks" doesn't seem to describe accurately eight acres of terra firma rising thirty feet out of the ocean. The best guess, therefore, is that a completely submerged channel between the headland and what *is* now an island was carved out sometime within the last two hundred years. The process is undoubtedly still going on, and the surf and current are munching away not only at the reef connecting the two bodies of land, but at Año Nuevo itself.

The physics involved in wave patterns and in the erosional force of refraction caused by breakers crashing into breakers is beyond my simple grasp of hydrology, but hydrology wasn't much on my mind when we motored out here this morning in the trusty Zodiac. Terror was on my mind. The crossing to Año Nuevo is most certainly not for the craven—particularly in winter. Strong winds and the Humboldt Current move from north to south along this stretch of the California coast; surf rolls into the channel, therefore, from the northwest. But the reef and the island are so close to the mainland that they create a kind of eddy or backflow at the southern end, resulting in an opposing line of surf rolling in from the south. Between these turbid distractions lies a choppy, shallow path about fifteen feet wide, which the feckless boatman negotiates at his peril. Misread the current, shear off a propeller, drift to the right or the left, and there are some alarming combers out there, fifteen feet of boiling brine waiting to gut and puree your little neoprene perambulator and masticate its cargo of fools like a handful of cocktail nuts.

One such cheerless event (chronicled in the *San Mateo County Gazette* for the 14th of April, 1883) involved some people one might suppose to be the *least* likely to suffer mishap—the lighthouse-keeper, his assistant, and two friends who visited them regularly from the mainland. The reporter's prose leaves room for improvement, but the story is certainly representative.

> One of the most appalling accidents that ever occurred on this coast, happened to Año Nuevo Island, twelve miles south of Pescadero, Sunday afternoon, April 8th, resulting in the death by drowning of four young men—Henry W. Colburn, Bernard A. Ashley, Clayton A. and Frank L. Pratt.

The Pratt brothers, the story explains, had spent a pleasant Sabbath with their lighthouse-keeper friends on the island, and all four were returning to the mainland at about 2:30 in the afternoon.

> Instead of taking the usual course—by the "beacon stake"—they started on what is known as the "straight cut." The distance in an air line is something more than half a mile. When about half the distance over, a heavy breaker partially filled the boat. Three of the occupants commenced bailing out the water, but before they had completed their task, another still heavier breaker swamped the boat, filling it with water. At this time all four of the men were sitting in the boat, which continued drifting out to sea until a heavy breaker rolled over them, and they disappeared from sight, which was the last ever seen of them.

Messrs. Colburn, Ashley, and Pratt were the first recorded victims of an accident in the channel, but they were by no means the last.

In 1948 the U.S. Coast Guard closed the lighthouse station, replacing the beacon and the air-powered diaphone (foghorn) with an automatic, 400-candlepower light and a radar reflector. Without constant maintenance the buildings began to deteriorate and fall apart; the metal beacon tower slowly rusted until it fell down in 1976; the catwalks that crossed from living quarters to light to foghorn station succumbed bit by bit to wind and rain and high seas; sea lions moved into the lightkeeper's house and gradually filled it with feces, molted fur, and corpses; the catchment basin cracked, buckled, and came apart. In 1958 the federal government finally decided to sell what it had come to regard as excess property, and the State of California, after a good deal of finagling, bought it for $52 thousand. What to do with it remained a question.

Given the island's fragile ecology, the sensitivity of its growing pinniped colonies to human intrusion, and the hazards presented by the channel, there was only one logical answer—close it to the public and turn it into a scientific reserve. It took nearly nine years to effect this solution officially, but in 1967 access was restricted to scientific users, and in 1968 the University of California, through its Natural Land and Water Reserves System, was granted a use permit to conduct studies of its seal and sea lion populations and to establish research facilities. A few observation blinds built by the Scientific Director and Manager of Physical and Life Sciences at the Stanford Research Institute, Dr. Thomas C.

Año Nuevo as seen from U.S. Highway 1.

California sea lions in abandoned lighthouse-keeper's house, Año Nuevo.

California sea lion trapped in fishing net.

Poulter, were already in place. Several new ones were added, the blockhouse was "renovated," and a privy was installed in a sandy swale a short distance away. Tonight it shall remain unvisited. No telling what one may encounter along the trail in the dark. At least the subadult down there in his cove is an audible presence by which I can find my way.

"Año Nuevo is the most important pinniped rookery and resting area in central and northern California," says Dr. Burney J. LeBoeuf, an authority on elephant seals and one of the principal investigators on the island since its affiliation with the University of California. "The magnitude of pinniped traffic on such a small place is staggering." Only two islands far to the south—San Miguel and San Nicolas—support a greater number of seals and sea lions, and both are considerably in excess of 9,000 acres. Año Nuevo, weighing in at about eighty acres, maintains a biomass that makes the others look diminutive. Counting elephant seals alone, for example, there were roughly 3,500 adults on its shore in 1984 as opposed to 20,000 on San Miguel. But in pounds per square foot, assuming an average animal weight of approximately 1,000 pounds, Año Nuevo could boast 218 tons per acre as opposed to one ton per acre for San Miguel. That is an accumulation of blubber of astonishing magnitude.

Four species share the rocky shelves and the two small beaches that comprise the island's perimeter—harbor seals, elephant seals, Steller's sea lions, and California sea lions. Of the latter two groups, distinguishable from true seals by small external ears and large foreflippers,* only the Steller's sea lions breed on Año Nuevo, and in numbers that have been decreasing since 1967 (though the population seems to have leveled off for the past few years). Steller's is the largest of the "eared" species. Males attain a weight of up to 2,000 pounds and can be easily spotted by the mane of golden brown hair that mantles their neck and shoulders. Females are similarly colored (light or golden brown when dry, almost grey when in the water), though they are only one-third as large and possess no mantle of guard hair.

Like all pinnipeds except the harbor seal, Steller's sea lions were hunted during the nineteenth century for their oil and hides. When that sport became commercially unprofitable in the late 1870s because of population depletion, a dollar could still be made from the genitalia of adult males, dried and powdered and sent off to China as an aphrodisiac. Their long whiskers were just dandy, moreover, for cleaning the sludge out of an opium pipe. Dog food was made out of the leftovers. At one time the most prevalent pinniped

*Seals are thought to have descended from an otterlike ancestor; sea lions from something more similar to a bear.

Southeast Farallon Island.

in California waters, Steller's ranged as far south as the Channel Islands; now Año Nuevo is the southernmost breeding place for this species. In 1967 there were 1,600 animals on the island; in 1984 only about 800. While that reduced population seems to have held reasonably steady for ten years, nobody knows if or when an exodus to the major rookeries that extend northward from British Columbia to the Aleutians may resume.

The California sea lion, smaller and considerably more common, breeds in southern waters and uses Año Nuevo only for rest and recuperation during a fall migration in search of food. Adult males are generally six to seven feet in length and weigh from 600 to 800 pounds; females are less than half that size and look as if they ought to be balancing a beach ball on the end of their nose—a feat they often perform in captivity. At peak season in September as many as 8,000 animals, almost all of them males, haul out and cover what will become in December elephant-seal territory. Their bark is familiar to anyone who has been to the circus, the zoo, or near the ubiquitous "seal rocks" that litter the Pacific coast; their sleek, porpoiselike appearance in the wake of boats trawling for salmon is discouragingly familiar to Monterey fishermen, many of whom shoot at them with a kind of dyspeptic pleasure.

By far the most impressive inhabitants of Año Nuevo, however, are the *compadres* of my noisy friend down there in the cove, snorting into his gullet and sounding like a Roman at the vomitorium—the northern elephant seal. Particularly the male northern elephant seal. Impressive not only because of his size (superbulls attain a length of 15 to 16 feet and weigh as much as 6,000 pounds); his preposterous proboscis, which hangs over a silly, misleading grin; and his bellicose behavior toward everything that interferes with his singleminded devotion to reproduction, but because his reproductive success is so demonstrably evident from one year to the next.

As a result of wholesale slaughter by nineteenth-century sealers, the worldwide population of northern elephant seals in 1892 was probably not greater than 100 animals and possibly as few as twenty. By 1977 the species had regenerated to 60,000, the result of protective legislation and a decline in the commercial uses of seal oil. But on Año Nuevo there were *no* elephant seals until 1955, when two females and two subadult males hauled ashore in late July, and no breeding activity until 1961, when a grand total of two pups were born. Seven years later, when I first visited the island with LeBoeuf, there were over 1,000; in 1980 about 1,200. Indeed, conditions in the Año Nuevo rookery had become so crowded by the end of the decade that a number of females had begun to cross to the mainland in search of calmer quarters to raise their young. A new colony started to form there, and in 1980 about 150 pups were born; in 1984 nearly 700.

For most of the year elephant seals stay entirely in the water, feeding, putting on the weight necessary to sustain a fast that will last throughout the breeding season. Males

Seabirds and sea lions on Año Nuevo, and the mainland coastline across the channel.

begin coming ashore during early December; females mid- to late December. Both will go without food or water until they depart, and throughout this period (34 days for females and up to three months for dominant males) they rely solely on the huge store of fat acquired during their nine months at sea.

They depart, one can be assured, a little lighter than they arrived. In addition to sustaining herself, a female nourishes her pup from an average birth weight of 83 pounds to a weaned weight four weeks later of about 300 pounds. While the weaner nearly quadruples in size (assuming it isn't drowned in a storm, or bitten to death for suckling at the wrong tap, or squashed by some two-ton Lothario in pursuit of his Jane), its mom deflates like a balloon, losing 800 to 900 pounds for her labors on the beach.

A dominant male fares no better. He may have the dubious honor of copulating 150 to 200 times in ninety days, but additional obligations come with the territory. He has to fight to maintain his position, enduring nasty bites from his opponents' canine teeth that leave him bloody if unbowed; he has to stay awake on the job, catching a catnap when he can, in order to avoid the humiliation of being cuckolded. When he finally hauls his bedraggled corpus into the ocean at the end of his spree, he is a listless shadow of his former self, several thousand pounds lighter, bushed, a far more vulnerable target for his only enemies, the great white shark and the killer whale.

As I stumble back from the foghorn building, drawn by the smell of mussels Chez LeBoeuf, I think about my belching, gagging chum down there in his narrow cove. If he lives to the ripe old age of nine, which he has less than a 20 percent chance of doing, he still has only a 50 percent chance at best of deflowering one of those beach blimps that so distract his mind. He may go to his maker wondering why he was ever brought onto this earth. He may, on the other hand, get lucky and become a superbull, may sire fifty pups a year for three or four years if he can find the work. It's pretty much all or nothing in the pinniped world.

Still, it is an expanding universe for *Mirounga angustirostris*—and that raises a few questions. Even with a high mortality rate among pups and subadult males, natural predation seems unable to cope with the exploding elephant seal population. As LeBoeuf puts it, unsentimentally, "How many elephant seals do we want?" Anticipating the day when pinniped and hominid come in conflict over space on the beach, he observes that "if the current growth rate continues, there will be thousands of elephant seals on the Año Nuevo mainland by the year 2000, and they will not remain on the state reserve." They are not interested, presumably, in the concept of multiple use. Well . . . this could prove amusing. Weaner pods and weenie roasts, harem and hoi polloi, all vying for the same seaside acreage. It might even provide an outlet for all those low-ranking males denied an official opportunity to reproduce but not at all fussy about the beneficiary of a peripheral copulation.

Weaned elephant seal pups, Año Nuevo.

People and supplies gain access to Southeast Farallon Island by crane for lack of landing sites.

I f one's interest is island avifauna rather than seals and sea lions, Año Nuevo is not a lively location to conduct research. Although the mainland reserve is extremely rich in the diverse species that use the area during their annual migration along the Pacific flyway, the scarcity of vegetation on the island, and the hazards of sharing habitat with oafish pinnipeds, seem to have restricted breeding activity to four bird species: pelagic cormorants, western gulls, a small number of pigeon guillemots (thirty to forty pair), and a few oystercatchers. If it's bird rookeries one is looking for, there is a better place nearby. The Farallons (*Los Farallones de los Frayles:* "little peaks of the friars"), lying as the crow flies about fifty miles to the northwest, will offer the seabird ornithologist everything he ever hoped for, short of permanent exile to the Pribilofs. *Los Farallones,* all 211 acres of them, are the largest North American seabird rookery south of Alaska.

Southeast Farallon Island, 65 acres of guano and granite poking up out of the California Current, is actually included within the boundaries of the County of San Francisco—though it lies some thirty miles out to sea and is closer to Bolinas in Marin County than to the City of the Golden Gate. Surrounded by satellite islets that nearly double its total size, it is the southernmost in a chain of peaks along a ridge of bedrock that roughly parallels the continental shelf from Cape Mendocino to south of Point Piedras Blancas. Middle Farallon, a single obstruction about 150 feet across and 20 feet high, lies about three miles to the northwest; North Farallon, six islets and a group of rocks, falls in line another four miles beyond. Only Southeast Farallon is "accessible."

Juan Cabrillo has often been credited with the "discovery" of these tiny islands, though no more concrete evidence supports this claim than supports the one that his bones lie interred beneath the sands of windswept San Miguel. The first written reference to their existence occurs in Sir Francis Drake's *The World Encompassed.* He calls them the Islands of Saint James and remarks that they provided his ship with a "plentiful and great store of seals and birds." Sebastián Vizcaíno noted them as a navigation mark for finding Punta de los Reyes (Point Reyes) and Drake's Bay, and various overland parties (Gaspar de Portolá in 1769 and Juan Bautista de Anza in 1776) recorded sighting their distant contours in their expedition journals.

It was Russian fur sealers, however, who first tried to inhabit the barren, exposed shelves of Southeast Farallon. In G. H. von Langsdorff's *Narrative of the Rezanof Voyage* a sealer named Chichinoff describes the pleasure of temporary settlement.

> A schooner took us down to the islands but we had to cruise around for over a week before we could make a landing. We had a few planks with us and some canvas, and with that scanty material and some sea-lion skins we built huts for shelter.

These jolly campers had 12 pounds of tea and 120 pounds of flour for provisions, no water but what they could find in the hollows of rocks, and no firearms. They killed sea

The Point Reyes Bird Observatory
research station on Southeast Farallon
Island.

Tufted puffin, Farallons.

"Contest for the eggs." *Harper's Monthly,* 1874.

lions with clubs, supplemented their meager diet with an occasional fish, and were soon reduced to eating seal meat. Only once in six months were they resupplied—another hundred pounds of flour and some tea—but Chichinoff and company were destined for harder times than they could imagine.

> About a month afterward the scurvy broke out among us and in a short time all were sick except myself. My father and two others were all that kept at work and they were growing weaker every day. Two of the Aleuts died a month after the disease broke out. All the next winter we passed there in great misery and when the spring came the men were too weak to kill sea lions, and all we could do was to crawl around the cliffs, and gather some sea-bird eggs and suck them raw.

In spite of such setbacks, seal hunters would eliminate pinnipeds from the island over the next thirty years. And while Chichinoff and friends couldn't know it, the eggs they sucked to keep themselves alive would soon replace fur as the object of a second great rape of the Farallons.

By 1830 the Farallon pinniped populations that once numbered hundreds of thousands of fur seals, sea otters, and northern elephant seals had been completely wiped out by the Russians and their Aleut serfs. * In 1849 Yankee ingenuity found something new to exploit. A man named "Doc" Robinson and his brother-in-law, Orrin Dorman, perceived that because San Francisco had no resident chickens, gold-rush trenchermen went without that staple of the breakfast board—*huevos rancheros.* They bought a boat. Robinson sailed it out to Southeast Farallon, gathered up about 3,000 murre eggs, and sold them on his return to the city for a dollar apiece. A day's wage for a day's work. But this gastronomic mother lode could hardly be kept a secret, and Robinson soon had plenty of company on his departures through the Golden Gate.

Between 1849 and 1881, nesting season (May through August) became egging season—and egging season was open season. A city that could consume 300,000 to 400,000 omelets during the three months of their availability could furnish a battalion of pickers to service its needs, and there were troops more than eager to volunteer. In short order unregulated harvesting began to impact the murre population in particular, but gull and cormorant numbers as well. The eggs of the latter two birds were less popular, though they would do in the absence of something better, and gulls suffered double abuse because

---

* The story of current pinniped diversity on Southeast Farallon is approximately the same as on Año Nuevo—California sea lions, Steller's sea lions, harbor seals, and elephant seals—though in total numbers Southeast Farallon accommodates less than one-fourth as many animals. Northern fur seals have been occasionally sighted on and around the islands, though no breeding has taken place since their nineteenth-century extermination. Sea otters, which have begun to repopulate Año Nuevo, have not extended their range farther north.

The Middle Farallons at sunset.

Biologist Larry Spear observing seabirds from blind on Southeast Farallon.

they were competitors for murre eggs. Their own offspring, pre- and postnatal, were
stepped on to curtail future pilfering. Now and then the egger population was impacted,
albeit minimally, when a greedy gatherer, his shirt loaded down with a couple hundred
embryonic murres, would pitch sunny side up off the slippery rocks and plunge like a
stone into the sea; but all things considered, the birds got the worst of it.

By the early 1890s the plundering of Farallon rookeries was finished. An annual
harvest that garnered as many as a half million eggs when the bonanza was first discovered
dwindled to fewer than 8,000 during the final years. More than 14 million unborn murres,
gulls, and cormorants had been scrambled, poached, boiled, baked, coddled, and fried;
the murre population alone declined over the half century from approximately 400,000
birds to about 20,000. The total number of gulls and Brandt's cormorants had been
reduced by 75 percent, and only forty double-crested cormorants remained out of a pre-
egging population of 5,000. Things were pretty quiet on Southeast Farallon.

Any recovery of avian and pinniped colonies on the Farallons is astonishing when

Breeding colony of common murres and Brandt's cormorants, Southeast Farallon Island.

"Gathering murre eggs on Farallon Island."
Harper's Monthly, 1874.

one considers its devastation during the nineteenth century. And sealers and eggers were not the only problems its native inhabitants faced. As on Año Nuevo, the federal government maintained a lighthouse station on Southeast Farallon, with four families living on the island until 1965. The presence of people, along with their dogs, cats, chickens, hogs, and a mule that reportedly enjoyed a surfeit of eggs with his daily forage, kept seabirds sufficiently disturbed that recolonization was limited and slow.

But, also as on Año Nuevo, the automation of the lighthouse in 1972 meant the removal of the last Coast Guard personnel and, except for routine maintenance of the aids to navigation, the transfer of caretaking responsibilities to a scientific organization operating under an agreement with the U. S. Fish and Wildlife Service—in this case the Point Reyes Bird Observatory, headquartered in Bolinas. The PRBO had established a research station on the island in 1968, but didn't take over as a "protective presence" until four years later.

The closure of the area essentially to all but research activity and the strict monitoring of movement through and around its various rookeries resulted in astonishing increases in murre, gull, and cormorant populations; the return of a breeding population of rhinoceros auklets, not seen since before the turn of the century; and significant growth in other breeding species such as the tufted puffin, Cassin's auklet, ashy storm-petrel, and pigeon guillemot. The island is now the largest western gull nesting ground in the world (35,000 birds); murres have quadrupled from their estimated 1890s low to somewhere around 80,000; Cassin's auklets, all 120,000 of them, literally sit shoulder to shoulder in their colonies. What this adds up to in grand figures is roughly 300,000 seabirds, on eighty-five acres of decomposed granite and *Lasthenia minor* ssp. *maritime*—commonly known as Farallon weed. It also means a lot of guano.

Much has been accomplished toward protection of the Farallon Islands from the kinds of abuses inflicted on its bird and marine mammal life in the past—federal protection as a National Wildlife Refuge and a National Marine Sanctuary, state protection as a California State Bird Refuge, designation by the State Water Resources Control Board as an Area of Special Biological Significance, limitations on access imposed by the Fish and Wildlife Service and the Point Reyes Bird Observatory. But whether our broadened awareness of ecological relationships and a heightened collective environmental consciousness can protect the regenerating Farallons from all threats posed by an industrialized world remains very much to be seen.

There are overt threats like the Reagan administration's recurrent proposals to lease the entire continental shelf for oil exploration and to "review" the bans on such activities within existing marine sanctuaries. There are also subtler threats like the unknown effects of radioactive-waste contamination and mainland pollutants such as chlorinated hydrocarbons, petroleum hydrocarbons, and heavy metals—all of which are present in

Black brant goose pauses to rest on Año Nuevo reefs during spring migration.

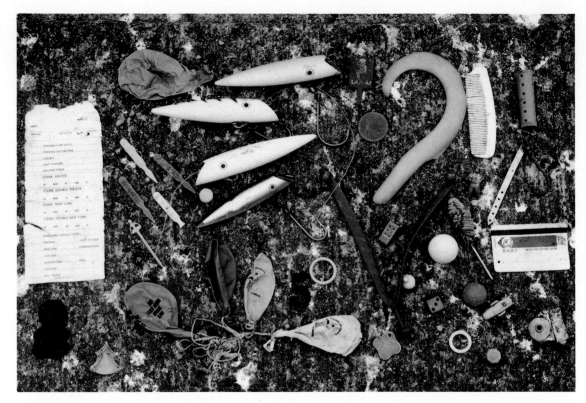

Items foraged from around San Francisco
Bay, collected from gull nests.

unaccountably high levels around the Farallons. Between 1946 and 1966 some 47,750
containers of radioactive waste were dumped within 4 to 14 miles of Southeast Farallon.
Twenty-five percent of the 55-gallon drums either imploded as they sank or rusted out
over time, resulting in fallout levels two to twenty-five times higher than the maximum
that would be expected from weapons-testing fallout. Scientists from the Lawrence Liv-
ermore Laboratory dispute the methodology used to arrive at these figures, and they
regard plutonium levels in Farallon fish and invertebrates as being "within global fallout
levels," but these cavils don't address the issue of whether such levels are acceptable or
answer the question, "Acceptable to whom?" Similar assurances were once made about
DDT, but no one in the pesticide business had brown pelicans or peregrine falcons in
mind when they assessed its "safety."

Environmental awareness is an essential component in the management and maintenance of wildlife populations on the Farallons, as it is on Año Nuevo or the Channel
Islands or any other place where the repercussions of human activities are felt. But envi-

ronmental awareness alone will not resolve anything. If we continue to dump our toxic wastes into the ocean, treating it with the same indifference and lack of understanding we afford most all our natural resources, then there seems little reason to believe we will be any more successful in preventing the degradation of our offshore ecosystems than we have been with the air we breathe or the land on which we live. Present conditions on the Farallons and Año Nuevo may give us reason to hope that enough of us are learning better, but we would be wise not to become too smug. As a prescription against complacency we might review, every morning upon rising, Aldo Leopold's admonishment of fifty years ago. "Twenty centuries of 'progress,'" he said, "have brought the average citizen a vote, a national anthem, a Ford, a bank account, and a high opinion of himself, but not the capacity to live in high density without befouling and denuding his environment, nor a conviction that such capacity, rather than such density, is the test of whether he is civilized."

GEM OF THE SAN JUANS

ORCAS ISLAND

*In the afternoon, to our great astonishment, we
arrived off a large opening extending to the
eastward, the entrance of which appeared to be
four leagues wide, and remained about that width
as far as the eye could see, with a clear westerly
horizon, which my husband immediately
recognized as the long lost strait of Juan de Fuca,
and to which he gave the name of the original
discoverer, my husband placing it on his chart.*

Mrs. Charles William Barkley, 1787

L ast ferry from Anacortes. I wedge my truck down into the boat's steel-plated
bowels with seventy or eighty other vehicles whose drivers are heading back to
their island homes, mostly pickups like mine and four-wheel-drive vans and middle-aged
American cars showing the rusty effects of sea weather and backcountry roads. Mostly
leathery old guys in billed caps with Coors and Caterpillar ads on the forepeak, and
women of indeterminate age in chino pants and quilted jackets, with the frazzled hair that
comes with misting rain and salt air. Few tourists this November evening.

Our course is due west, across the Rosario Strait and through the narrow pass between
Blakely and Decatur, north toward the tip of Lopez Island, and on to the terminal at
Orcas. Rain spatters the windows of the passenger salon, and the glass steams over on
the inside. Dampness dogs me wherever I go. I stand wiping my vaporized breath from
the glass, trying to see across the flat grey water to the headlands that lie scattered in heavy
mist across the straits. At low tide off this part of the Washington coast, this northernmost

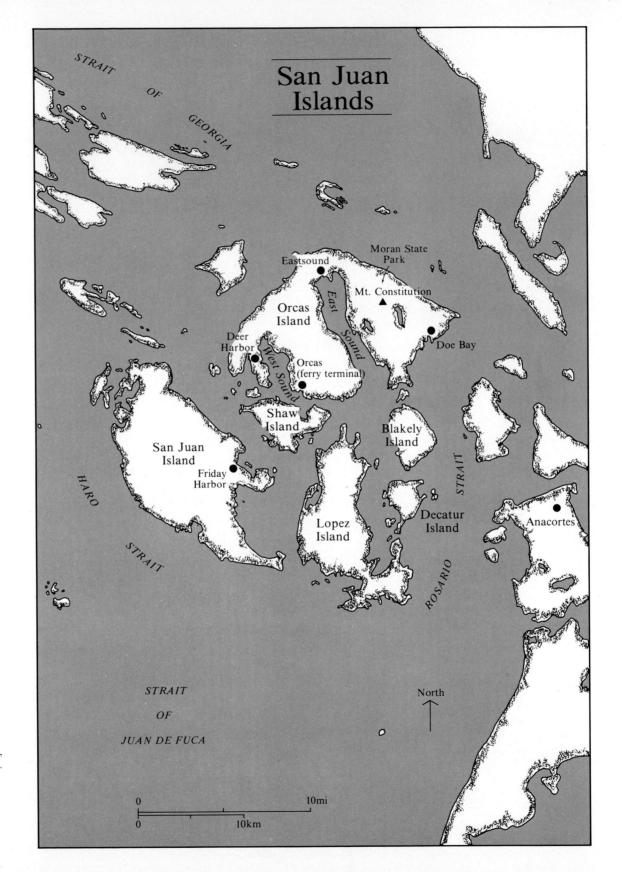

San Juan Islands

STRAIT

OF

GEORGIA

Moran State Park

Eastsound

Mt. Constitution ▲

Orcas Island

East Sound

Deer Harbor

West Sound

Doe Bay

Orcas (ferry terminal)

Shaw Island

Blakely Island

San Juan Island

Friday Harbor

HARO

STRAIT

Lopez Island

Decatur Island

ROSARIO

STRAIT

Anacortes

North ↑

STRAIT

OF

JUAN DE FUCA

0   10mi

0   10km

Page 78: The view from Mount Constitution, looking northwest towards Vancouver Island.

tip of the lower United States, 768 fragments of a dying mountain range reach above the Pacific; at high tide only 457. Black crags with mossy hems, bony reefs, dark green hills clambering up in a desperate attempt to escape the attention of time and wind and water. Of the 457, only 172 bear names, though all carry the general apellation San Juan Archipelago. Orcas, San Juan, and Lopez islands contain three-quarters of the total land area.

Down in Seattle they call this region the banana belt because it is protected from Pacific storms by the Olympic Range to the southwest and Vancouver Island to the northwest; it receives, in some places, as little as 20 inches of rainfall a year. But this evening we have no bananas. We have clouds hunkered down on the water and a cold rain blowing horizontally from the Strait of Georgia to the north. We have a grumpy traveller wishing his amphibious parking lot would arrive at Orcas, where presumably bed and board await him—and perhaps a toddy or two.

Orcas. In the early nineteenth century it was a winter settlement for the Northwest's Lummi Indians, a gentle, nomadic group of fish and berry eaters who are remembered chiefly for the ease with which they were pushed around by the southward-raiding Haidas from Queen Charlotte Sound, and the ease with which they were "relocated" by the white men who first drifted down from Canada's Fraser River gold country around 1840.

Peering through my steamy window I can almost see them out there, those Lummi, pulling without gain through the cross-hatch of wind and current, their canoes rearing in the chop that blows diagonally across the narrows, their women and children woven between their legs, hiding from the spray and cutting breath of the storm. They bear off the wind, plying sideways to break free of the dangerous stricture of currents, finally reach a pass between shadowed land masses, and pull around the point into the shelter of a long fiord. The canoes slide inland, eight miles up the waterway that nearly dissects the island and makes it appear from above like a pair of tattered lungs, to the shell-whitened beach where they disembark. When the storm passes, the women gather on the exposed, sodden flats, stoop, and dig with their fingers. Horse and butter clams, cockles, geoducks, mussels. They drop them in woven baskets, pausing as they straighten to chatter quietly, or watch a flock of ducks dive for smelt. The men have gone to Peapod Rocks, between Point Lawrence and Doe Bay, to stretch their reef nets for salmon, and the children have scattered inland to pick blackberries and gather wood for the evening fires.

Orcas is the largest and most varied of the San Juan Islands, 56 square miles of land, 125 miles of coast, thickly wooded, gouged by watery incisions. The soil of its slopes is a dark-complexioned union of recycled vegetation, volcanic ash, glacially worn magma— a soil so laden with potential that it seems to explode in a profusion of jungly vines, ferns, berry bushes, soft maple, alder, marsh willows, tamarack, hemlock, cedar, spruce, Douglas fir; all of it massing upward toward the cone of Mount Constitution, elevation 2,400 feet and the highest point in the archipelago, where an assembly of white pines stand like pillars around a gallery of Northwest seascapes, landscapes, cloudscapes. As any resident of the island will tell you, the view from Mount Constitution is "breathtaking."

They will also tell you that the weather is not as it currently appears to be. Although the mainland climate is raw, the San Juans are distributed throughout an area where temperatures hover at a cool 70 degrees F in summer and in winter rarely descend below 40 degrees F. Storms move swiftly over, and more often around, the islands, dropping only "enough" rain as they head for their real destinations: the Cascades to the east, the Olympic Range on the peninsula to the south, Vancouver Island across the Strait of Haro to the west. When the surrounding land masses are socked in with fog, the view from Orcas is wide and blue and bright.

So my persecution by the elements is apparently exclusive. Precipitation seems to follow me the way gulls hound a garbage scow. When I am finally tucked into bed in my comfy cabin in Deer Harbor, well wined and reasonably dined, the rain drums so heavily on my roof that I cannot sleep, and I am forced to read. Loathsome pastime. I thumb through assorted pamphlets, local historical society publications, and the diary of an early settler, James Francis Tulloch. History. A fire of somewhat damp spruce limbs hisses and pops in the fireplace, and I tell myself I have definitely not started smoking again as I light up a cheap, fat cigar. Not to be inhaled, this.

At the end of the eighteenth century a number of Spanish and English expeditions, as well as several American trade vessels, entered the Strait of Juan de Fuca and prowled Puget Sound. De Fuca, a Greek seaman with a lively imagination, claimed to have discovered the opening to this inland waterway in 1592—claimed, in fact, to have sailed along it all the way from the Pacific to a sea that he thought was either the Arctic or the Atlantic. A remarkable feat, although as Bernard DeVoto remarked, "This strait too [like the Strait of Anian] was accepted, laid down on maps, sought for, and sometimes traveled by other liars." Whether or not the Greek navigator was ever in the vicinity of the 49th parallel, it was the Spanish who directed the most attention to exploration of the area in the beginning, mapping its perimeters and naming a great many of its features. However, an English lieutenant, William Broughton (under Captain George Vancouver), first crept through the labyrinthine inner sanctum of this sinking continent where the larger Spanish ships were unwilling to go, and in 1841 Captain John Wilkes, charged by the United States Congress with the enormous task of surveying the coasts of America, sailed into the San Juans and began charting them for Uncle Sam.

No doubt by the time Wilkes reached the Northwest he had exhausted his bucket of appropriate names. Perhaps his very lateness in coming aroused in him a territorial belligerence. Whatever the case, Wilkes renamed every island, every filament of water, every conspicuous aspect of the archipelago; and the drabness of his imagination was exceeded only by the utter thoroughness with which he affixed names to objects in spite of their

Sun burning through morning fog, Orcas.

Fishing boats, Friday Harbor, San Juan Island.

obvious discord with the shapes and textures they attempted to describe. Navy Archipelago, Rogers Island, Hull Island, President Channel, Mount Constitution. Fortunately some of the Spanish names withstood the captain's salute to his benefactors. Orcas (Wilkes's Hull) undoubtedly derives not from the Roman god but from the Spanish word for the killer whales that school throughout the islands. Petty boosters, the small of spirit, might complain that there is no good reason for Spanish names to abound in the Pacific Northwest, and that travel agents tend to confuse the region with the capital of Puerto Rico, but I experience no such discomfort. Neither did Mr. Curtis, founder of the mainland town of Anacortes, the place whence the ferry boats come. He named his settlement after his wife—Ann Curtis—and then latinized it to Ana Cortes.

Up with the first shaft of sunlight slanting through the separation in the curtains; up, not because I'm eager to crawl out on this frosty morning but because I can't believe the transformation from storm to not-storm. I'm worried about the bends. The tiny port of Deer Harbor is completely deserted, the slips and moorings empty at this time of year,

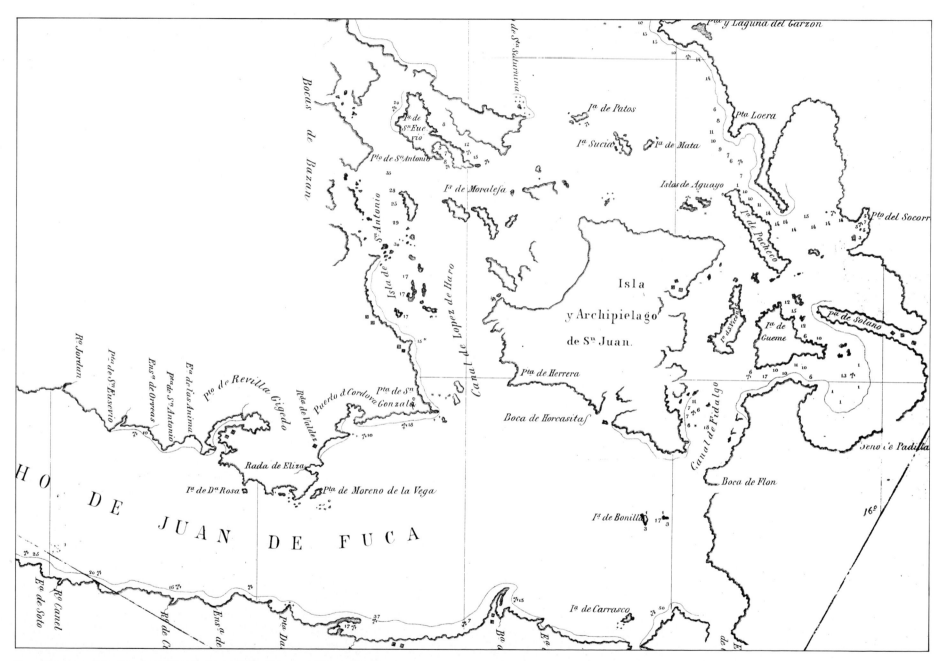

Spanish map of the San Juan Islands from 1791. Courtesy Bancroft Library.

the bait shop closed. I walk to the end of the gas dock, feeling my way carefully over the frozen boards, sliding my hand along the rime ice of the railing, and watch the shorebirds already busy in the tide flats. They poke here and there with their pointed little beaks, extracting whatever it is that passes for bacon and eggs if you're a sandpiper, then skitter back from a lapping wavelet like a record programmed for a slower speed suddenly played at 78 rpm. The sun is just striking the tops of the spruce on the hill across the harbor. Madrona trees tilt drunkenly over the bank to my left, their yellow trunks shining wetly, lacquered and smooth as Chinese boxes.

I can imagine this place 150 years ago when the first few French Canadian trappers began to percolate down through the San Juans in search of beaver, mink, and raccoon. Lone men. Ragged miners drifting back down from the Fraser River without gold or hope or home. Sailors who jumped the big naval ships. More trappers, after the Hudson's Bay Company opened a trading post on San Juan Island in 1845; trappers who wiped out the beavers by 1850 through the mindless destruction of their dams, and so depleted the brown mink population that not enough could be trapped to sell, and who were finally reduced to slaughtering the rampant, less valuable deer for their hides, wasting the meat. Men who quarried lime, or cut wood for the kilns above Cascade Lake and along the rocky shores. Smugglers of opium, liquor, and Chinese labor, who capitalized on the islands' proximity to the Canadian border, and whose job was made easy by the myriad hidden coves and networks of channels. Lone men, a few of whom, having heard of or seen the islands, came expressly to start a new life, a family, a community.

Why did they stay? They had the whole of Washington Territory at their disposal; fertile, sweeping land, like the Skagit River valley, or growing centers of commerce such as the Port of Seattle, or the huge mill operations on the Olympic Peninsula. Why these little islands with their flimsy communications, travel routes that were not only laborious but risky, and nonexistent female population? Who knows? Perhaps because it was a smaller, more precise existence. Perhaps because it *wasn't* without limits, but was qualified by watery borders. A man could see the boundaries of his world, and between the two, the man and the source, a kind of understanding had a chance to grow. That's in large part what we in-migrants are after today; why not then?

And also, within the perimeters of this world, there was abundance and the promise in soil, water, and weather of more abundance. I talk with a local fisherman outside the Outlook Inn, where I go for lunch, and along with the information that last night's storm was the worst in thirty-five years, and some laconic observations about the salmon run this year, he remarks, "As long as the tide goes out you can't starve in the San Juans." If that is true now, it was certainly truer a hundred years ago. A man could not starve as long as the tide gave access to the clams and oysters and mussels that were everywhere for the taking, nor could he go thirsty with artesian springs and freshwater lakes sprinkled

Signpost along Lopez Island's main road.

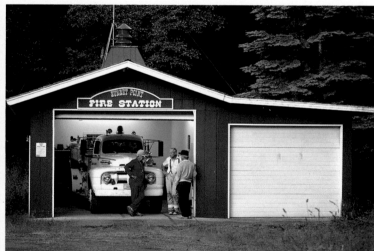

Sunset Point Fire Station, San Juan Island.

Toolmaker Gregg Blomberg examines an adze blade, Lopez Island.

British camp, San Juan Island, circa 1866–71.
Courtesy Provincial Archives of British Columbia.

here and about, nor could he die of exposure on those tree-thick slopes that provided all the wood for fires and shelter he'd ever need. There was, in a way, little to grapple with. Nature was *for* him in the islands.

Whatever the reasons, they stayed. The earliest bought squaws and married them— not Lummi women, thought inferior because they were too docile, but daughters of the northern tribes. A few all-white families arrived, cleared the land, and used the small logs to build homes. They planted apples and pears and prunes, wheat and hay, gardens of peas and potatoes; raised sheep on the mountainsides, and hogs and chickens in their backyards; fished for salmon, ling and rock cod, and halibut; hunted quail, duck, pheasant, and deer; picked berries and hazelnuts; drank black-currant wine; danced; bore children; erected churches. In that order.

Late in the afternoon I walk along the coastline that runs south from Deer Harbor toward the point and Pole Pass, between Crane Island and Orcas. A half-dozen crows are mixing it up in the middle of the road, outdoing one another in a cantankerous debate over who gets what in reference to the defunct cat somebody's truck tire has pasted to

American camp (from an old drawing), San Juan Island. Courtesy Provincial Archives of British Columbia.

the macadam. They regard my passing in sullen silence from a nearby stand of pines, then flap back to their salubrious meal (if you happen to be a crow) in my wake. The road bends through the woods; emerges on open pastureland and the remnants of an apple orchard. The trees are laden with fruit, the ground beneath them littered with windfalls, and although I am a timid trespasser, I don't mind if I do. Thank you very much.

For most of the Orcas farmers in the late nineteenth century, the island's calling was fruit, and its *coup de maître,* apples. In the spring one could stand on almost any of these hills and let one's gaze slide down across rows of white, fluttery blossoms as regular as pearls laid out on a carpet of loam-black velvet; in the fall, the trees dark green and the ground sequined with sweet windfall. From the docks at Eastsound, 160,000 boxes a year passed into the holds of the eight steamers that served the islands and mainland ports. The land made good on its promise. But it wasn't enough. The depression of 1891 that closed the banks brought down a number of Orcas fruit growers; competitors from eastern Washington with cooperative marketing and grading techniques, better transportation, and prettier apples brought down the rest. By the end of World War One the orchards were abandoned, the stores closed, the docks in disrepair, and the farmers who handled staples were also losing their market to the more easily maneuvered crops of the mainland.

For those whose lifestyle and occupation did not challenge the obvious fact that islands have limited accessibility, those who relied on resources particular to the islands, surviving the progress of other regions was not impossible. Lime-quarry workers, at one point, saw 25,000 barrels a year roll out of the towering stone kilns. There was wood to be cut from the mountainsides behind the quarries to feed the kilns. There were fish to be netted and delivered to Orcas's own cannery at Deer Harbor, or salted and shipped to mainland ports. And there was always sailing, first on freight and passenger steamers, later on the ferries that began serving Washington Sound in 1922. And, of course, during the 1920s smuggling was an honorable profession with a considerable tradition. Lookouts on peaks, signal fires by night, dark boats sliding by in the lee of fogbound points, trucks (backed by huge Seattle contraband corporations) waiting at prearranged landings. During Prohibition smuggling became everyone's avocation, and smugglers the equivalent of the weekend broker. But in the end the mainland won. The lime kilns declined, the packing houses were relocated, the Volstead Act was repealed. The islands were left with but one surviving industry worthy of the name. Tourism. Whether the islands will survive the surviving industry is an open question.

There are no dining facilities open at Deer Harbor once the season has ended, and while there is a kitchen in my cabin I'm in the mood to avoid my own cooking. I drink a silent toast to the departing sun and climb into the pickup, driving the eleven miles into the village of Eastsound along Crow Valley Road. Hayfields fall off on either side of me like pale green veils, and the day's warmth slips through the open window in a mix of smells—clover, leaf mold, sourwood, cow barn. Occasionally a modest sign informs me that "unique" pottery and stoneware can be purchased if I will just turn onto this or that retreating road. The ubiquitous arts and crafts. California transplants, I bet.

At the Outlook Inn I sit once again among nineteenth-century clapboard, polished antiques, pewter, brass, flowered wallpaper. A pretty young waitress with smooth, heavy hair and a long Victorian gown serves me homemade soup from an ironware pot, fresh bread, baked salmon, and picture-bright vegetables. There are no other customers, but the Inn looks as if it were preparing for a Mormon family reunion, all tables set, each little lamp blushing amber, the kitchen sending feasty smells from room to room. I order coffee and the deep-dish apple pie with ice cream, figuring the only thing worse than a coronary is half a coronary, but my rosy-cheeked attendant comes back to tell me they

Islet off San Juan Island.

are out of the deep-dish apple pie. "Spared," I say, and she smiles. I ask her where people go on Orcas when they really want to put on the dog, and inaccurately fingering me for a dull, middle-aged tourist instead of the hipster I really am, she says, "Rosario." It's the third time I've heard it. "Oh, you've got to go out to Rosario and Moran State Park. The view from Mount Constitution is . . . breathtaking."

Robert Moran was the local Medici. He came here in 1904, desperately ill, a prosperous shipbuilder with six months to live (according to his doctors), and died thirty-nine years later after erecting various monuments to himself, not all of which might please him greatly today. Moran and Orcas seemed to have struck a bargain. In exchange for those thirty-nine bonus years he donated to the commonwealth one mountain and a paved road to its summit (after having bought the land, patch by patch, from discouraged settlers), and erected a tri-level family mansion on Cascade Bay, a mansion whose construction was so meticulously wrought that it inspired public tours. It featured a foundation hewn from bedrock, two concrete stories and a third framed from wood, the interior finished with imported teakwood and mahogany, a copper-sheeted roof, a basement pool, a bowling alley, billiard tables, a music room with a 1,972-pipe organ, squeakless hinges of Moran's own design, stained glass from Brussels, and so on and so on. The house and its surrounding 1,000 acres, ornamental lagoon, boat docks, gardens, hydroelectric plant, and machine shops were renamed, through Moran's petition, Rosario. Originally it had been the small lumber community of Newhall.

A man's home is his castle. Why begrudge him its design? Besides, Moran kept most of Orcas employed through the Depression, and he bought an additional 5,000 acres of lakes, forests, and Mount Constitution, all of which he gave to the state for a permanent preserve. But when Moran's wife died he sold Rosario to a retired Californian (of course), who lived in it for a while and sold it to a Texas company (of course), which hacked up much of the estate's hillsides and built speculation homes on postage-stamp lots before selling it once again to a Gilbert Geiser & Company, which converted the mansion into a . . . Re-zort!

And, oh my, look at it now. We got "villas," and "haciendas," and "cabanas," and a "boatel." We got a landing ramp for seaplanes, three swimming pools, tennis courts, gift shops and boutiques, beauty salons, restaurants (one of which is tiered five deep against a view window like a stack of aquariums). We got dance combos and disco, lawn games for the kiddies, runabouts for the fishermen, floats for the yachtsmen, "get-acquainted" cocktail parties for the lonely, "Mid-Week Unwinders" for the tryster and adulterer, "Island Get-Aways" for the conventioneer without portfolio. The resort's expressed purpose is to "insulate your psyche" and give you a "Treasure Island," but like the old hooker whose make-up begins to run under all those hot lights, it undoes by overdoing. Whatever natural appeal it might once have had has been reduced to hollow, jangly, expensive

Harbor seal swimming.

Tidelands, Orcas.

noise. At least that's my unbiased opinion. I won't spend any of my well-pinched pennies here.

My well-pinched pennies, according to a real-estate broker I talk with in Eastsound, will turn over eight times before they leave Orcas no matter where I spend them. And the Rosario Resort accounts for ten percent of the county's tax base, he says—a tax base that reached $12.30 per thousand in 1978 and continues to spiral. "So our resorts are a double bonus. They not only pay big taxes, they bring visiting dollars to other business. And I'll tell you something else, my friend, a lot of people who come here for a vacation come back to buy a second home."

Well, he *is* in real estate. Other people I talk with aren't quite so sure about the benefits of the visiting dollar. The visiting dollar may provide the wherewithal for extra services, like an extra deputy sheriff, or a gifted-student program at the local high school, or regular San Juan Airline flights to and from the islands; they may attract specialized industries such as entertainment, crafts, a pro shop for the golf course, a once-a-week TV repairman from Anacortes; but they also generate a *need* for these services that wasn't there in the first place. The ferries are often so crammed that residents, some of whom must commute, wait four and five hours to get off the island, then wind up stranded on the mainland when they want to return. Nonresidents pinch off forty percent of the sheriff's energy, whose decathlon *local* responsibilities include medical aid, removing pigs from the roads, directing cattle traffic, checking on isolated senior citizens who refuse to abandon what remains of their failing homesteads (after they have parcelled them off to buy food and pay taxes), chopping up jellyfish reported to be stinging swimmers, rescuing lost hunters. No wonder an extra deputy is needed.

It's the same old problem. People mean growth, and growth, to some people, means progress. To a few people, profits; to most, higher taxes and fewer amenities. Referring to tourism, a San Juan County commissioner once declared, "That's one good industry I think we can have here. One that's easy to live with." What he really meant is live *off*—which is unfortunate because tourism is seasonal and ephemeral, and tourists are transients with no vested interest in maintaining the natural ambience of the places they visit. More often than not, tourism is simply a preamble to vacation-home development. Everywhere I go on Orcas there is early evidence of that.

Above water the island still retains pretty much the shape of its first incarnation. But for how long? Already builders with the right equipment and the right money have begun crawling up the ridges. Between Point Lawrence Road and the lower park limits of Mount Constitution, sunlight flashes off windows that peer through jagged breaches in the old, somber firs. Big boxy homes, the carpenter's chalk marks still visible on the wood, queue up along Deer Harbor Road, hoping for a peek at the scenery. Along the cliff side of that recently tarred road only a narrow strip of root ground remains for the

Water ouzel, Cascade Creek, Orcas.

Douglas firs, Moran State Park, Orcas.

Mausoleum, San Juan Island.

madrona whose branches twist out over the shore rocks below. Half-acre lots sell for anywhere from $10 thousand to $50 thousand: houses, $50 thousand to $300 thousand. Not exactly a low-rent retreat, but then it's absolutely amazing how many people there are in this world with a lot of money. And they don't all wear suits and ties either.

I hike along the road that circumnavigates West Sound, Orcas's second deepest inlet. The maples on the banks are turning, their outer leaves flaring red and yellow against the backdrop of cool spruce. Snowberry bushes sway in the whoosh of a passing car. A young man with long hair and a rattletrap pickup full of carpenter's tools slows, raises his eyebrows in question. Sure. I'll take a ride. I want to ask him about construction on the island and he doesn't look like somebody who's going to give me a real-estate broker's pitch.

He doesn't. He talks about limits. He is, naturally, an in-migrant from California (via Oregon), building his own house on a half-acre lot over near Terrill Beach. He confesses with a smile that the land was given to him by his father-in-law; otherwise he could not have afforded it. And he talks, in a hopeful, nonstop monologue, about the Comprehensive Plan (San Juan County's first effort to regulate development), twenty-acre, five-acre, and base densities, sewer systems and building-permit moratoriums imposed by the lack thereof, open-space tax incentives, a group called HOPE (Help Orcas Preserve its Environment). He talks with irritation about absentee landlords, Bellingham syndicates, and inveterate islanders who believe they possess inalienable rights to subdivide and build whatever they choose on their own property. Like many in-migrants (and an increasing number of natives) he has learned to listen for the earliest sputterings of uncontrolled growth; and the real-estate signs, surveyors' flags, and new dirt roads rutted by heavy-equipment treads make a blip on his radar screen long before they disturb the more complacent old-timer, who doesn't altogether believe that the twenty-first century will ever invade his space.

It already has, of course, and not only by make-a-buck-and-split artists but by their antithesis—as my driver himself is evidence. Other articulate voices, such as the *Lopez Island Recorder,* are opposing uncontrolled growth in the islands, and recently there has been a shift by the county commissioners in favor of planning. The tiny island of Waldron rose up almost *en masse* and defeated a development proposal, and then initiated the first Nature Conservancy project in the Pacific Northwest. The Comprehensive Plan that my driver is so enthusiastic about has been accepted by all the islands, though Orcas, apparently more solidly in the hands of real-estate developers, stonewalled on the whole business and tried to opt out. So there is hope—at least until the pendulum swings again

Cedar foliage, Orcas Island.

Real-estate developer's sign, San Juan Island.

and the growth-progress-lunch-bucket proponents blow the environmental circuit-breakers with cries of economic deprivation, depression, and bureaucratic interference with our personal freedom.

The lines are not simply drawn, and the sentiments underlying commitment to one side or the other are as complicated and varied as human nature itself. In one of the seven real-estate offices I wander into in Eastsound, an elderly man in pressed overalls is stapling insulation to the walls of his newly expanded building and chatting at the same time with a Yakima couple about the property they have just bought. The couple examine a map spread out on his desk while he rambles on about the first family who owned the land, what they grew on it, why the son who inherited it (a school chum of his own son) left it for more opportune climes. He is a third-generation islander, he says, and you can hear in the way he pronounces the names of homesteaders and their children and the unreal places they have moved to that he loves his homeland and all the personal engravings it has made on his sixty-odd years. Yet here he is, part and parcel of a booming mill whose grist is land, whose object is profit, and whose environmental byproducts he studiously ignores.

He doesn't talk about limits. He doesn't talk about the overload new development has put on the power supply to the islands: a submarine, high-voltage cable from the Bonneville Dam on the Columbia River that can carry only so many kilowatts or megawatts or whatever kind of watts before it will brown out. Fourteen hundred compulsory "demand meters" have recently been installed in Orcas homes to "encourage" conservation, and it has been strongly suggested that large consumers of power, like the Rosario Resort, install automatic load-controlling devices that will shut down the least required appliances when demand exceeds load-limit capacity.

He doesn't talk about water limits either, and maybe there isn't much of a problem yet; but I read in my breakfast paper that Eastsound water users will have their regular meeting at 7:30 in the Realty Office, and I wonder why, if there is no problem, they have a regular meeting. On page three of that same paper I read an ad for a "Professional Water Witch—Urgently Needed. Beginning salary, $20,000. Rapid advancement." It occurs to me that the issue is perhaps not so much a paucity of water witches, but of water. Clean water. Water unpolluted by leaking septic tanks. Because I also read that sewage treatment, or rather the inadequacy of it, is a major issue in the populated center of the settlement. Welcome to the twenty-first century.

One tour around the island before the last ferry to Anacortes and the drive home. And I might as well admit it, I've got to check out that view from Mount Constitution. The road winds up the mountainside through dense woods, pops out into rocky clearings for quick, postcard previews of the panorama to come, ducks back under a canopy of delicate maple and alder. A parking lot. A trail leading to the stone lookout tower built during the Depression by the CCC. It's like a little cairn on the highest point of the summit, the highest point in the archipelago, up above the tiny island, above the tree tops, above everything; a 360-degree cinerama, sense-surround, worldscape that is . . . well, it's a vast, interminable, unimaginable space without fore- or middleground, without point of reference, nothing but whirligig distance and the sound of wind in my ears. To the east, the white cone of Mount Baker towering above the mainland haze; to the south, the Strait of Juan de Fuca and the Olympic Range, snowcapped peaks jutting above the purple wash of mountain wall; to the west, islands, water, islands, water, islands; to the north, Canada, Vancouver, the Queen Charlottes.

But I leave my camera hanging around my neck, reminding myself of all those negatives in my drawer back home of mind-blowing vistas from places like the Grand Canyon, Mount Whitney, the Gobi Desert; Pentax dioramas without subject or composition, nothing, in fact, but wide-angle space, a carousel of breathtaking transparencies, memories in Kodacolor, cherished moments along the trail. Impossible to record. Next slide, please.

WHALES AND EAGLES
VANCOUVER ISLAND

We were now threatened with a fog and a
storm, and I wanted to get into some place to
stop the leak before we encountered another
gale. These reasons induced me to steer for an
inlet, which we had no sooner reached than
the weather became so foggy that we could not
see a mile before us . . .

Captain James Cook, 1778

Jim Borrowman backs the *Gikumi* away from the pier while his partner, Bill Mackay, secures the herring tender being towed behind the bigger boat. Frans Lanting tries to explain to a hopeful collection of photography students that the heavy fog obscuring the northern end of Vancouver Island, Queen Charlotte Sound, the Johnstone Strait, British Columbia, Canada, and for all I know the entire North American continent is really terrific for taking pictures of intertidal organisms, and that the rain falling through the fog from the worldwide cloud mass above won't be a problem either, because the cameras will be pointed down, not up. Privately he concedes that everyone is going to get wet regardless, this being a part of the world where precipitation might better be measured in feet than inches—twenty to twenty-five feet a year over on the northwest coast of the island.

Telegraph Cove, looking more like a movie set for a romantic comedy than the tiny boat launch and sawmill community it is, recedes from our stern and suddenly vanishes

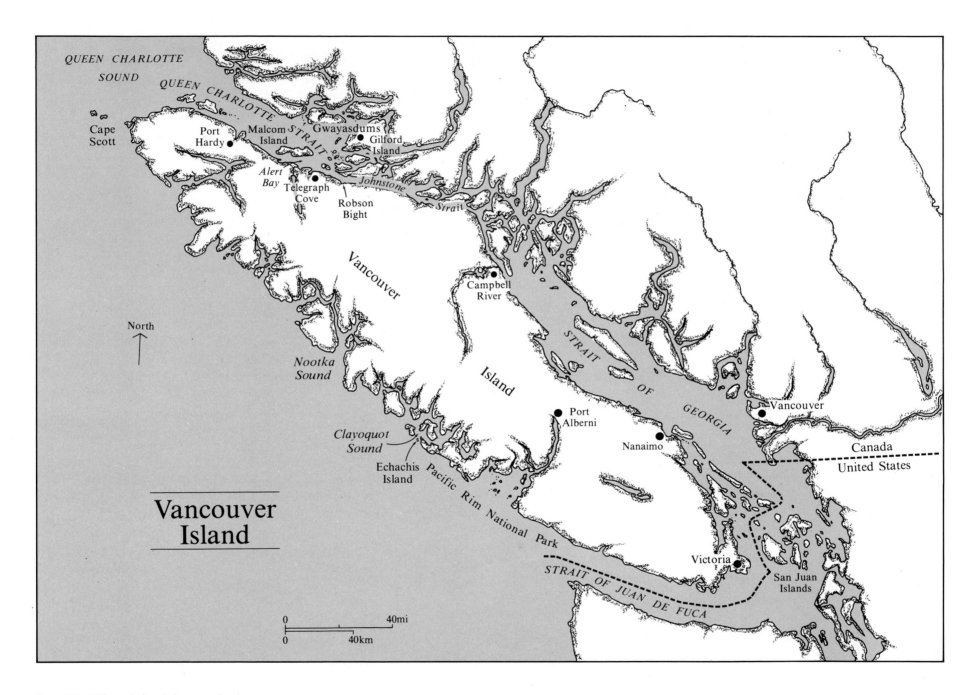

QUEEN CHARLOTTE SOUND

QUEEN CHARLOTTE STRAIT

Cape Scott

Port Hardy

Malcom Island

Gwayasdums

Gilford Island

Alert Bay

Telegraph Cove

Robson Bight

Johnstone Strait

Vancouver

Campbell River

North

Nootka Sound

Island

STRAIT OF GEORGIA

Vancouver

Clayoquot Sound

Port Alberni

Nanaimo

Canada

United States

Echachis Island

Pacific Rim National Park

Vancouver Island

Victoria

San Juan Islands

STRAIT OF JUAN DE FUCA

0   40mi

0   40km

Page 100: Killer whales, Johnstone Strait.

in the drifting mist. We turn left and head across the straits toward the myriad islands that swarm around the mouth of Knight Inlet, a long fiord that extends eighty or ninety miles into the British Columbia mainland. As if on cue the fog lifts for a moment at Stubbs Island to reveal three bald eagles, one of them immature and lacking the hoary locks of seniority, glaring at us from the snags of a geriatric tree. Flocks of phalaropes skim the placid waters of the sound, and a pair of rhinoceros auklets beat by on short, frenzied wings. They look poorly designed for flight, like little pinioned torpedoes.

Behind us the steep mountains of the northern coast rise a mile high through vertical layers of wispy cloud, their forested slopes so dense it is hard to imagine how a single tree, whether toppled by age or a chainsaw, could ever fall to the ground—a lumber company argument for clearcutting, in fact, and this is lumber country with a vengeance. Mile after mile of wilderness skinned clean as a whistle, some of it burned over to encourage new growth, some of it replanted, some of it looking like the aftermath of the *Enola Gay*. Along the one and only highway that runs up from Victoria at the island's southern end to Port Hardy at its northern end (a distance of more than 300 miles) the effects of unrestricted logging are clearly visible from any seat on the bus—indeed are inescapable, particularly past the town of Campbell River, where the road turns inland through the Nimpkish Valley. One imagines God's own straight-edge descending through the firmament and shaving Douglas fir off the mountain cheeks like a man mowing his Monday morning whiskers. It's not much different below Campbell River, for that matter, but here the road parallels the Strait of Georgia, and the motor homes towing fishing boats are so thick that one's eye rarely strays from the center line.

Tourism and forest products. Over 90 percent of Vancouver Island is covered with trees—hemlock, red cedar, white pine, lodgepole pine, spruce, balsam, yew, alder, and the remnants of once great stands of Douglas fir. And 90 percent of the trees are leased to lumber companies by the provincial government. Most of the towns, with the exception of those along the tourist strip from Victoria to Campbell River, are company towns, and when it's hard times in the woods, it's hard times for nearly half the island residents. When MacMillan–Bloedel shut down four of its mills in 1982, one out of three workers in Port Alberni was out of work. Twelve thousand people sat around waiting for a renaissance in the American building trades and a revival of the North American pulp market.

Catering to the modern outdoorsman in his eighteen-wheel RV, with the flush toilet, air conditioning, microwave oven, and three-jet whirlpool bath, seems to be Vancouver Island's alternative to a fickle forest-products economy. The outdoorsman, generally positioned under a baseball cap advertising somebody's lumberyard or farm machinery or alcoholic beverage, and generally towing a 25-foot Bayliner with a fully instrumented flying bridge and an inboard-outboard powerplant big enough to drive a PT boat, can be found clogging the highway, along with hundreds of his compeers, from late spring to late fall. As one local put it: "This place goes national in the summer. It's not our world from June to September. It takes to November before anything feels normal again."

International might be more accurate. Victoria suffers from such unrelieved anglophilia that it is often difficult to see past the tweed and tartan to enjoy the floral luxury of its natural environment, but driving north is a true excursion to the land of polyglot, the worst of which seems to have been imported from America. The weary traveller need not forego his Egg McMuffin or his Big Mac. Colonel Sanders is waiting to serve him his nine-piece order of extra-crispy, complete with sugared coleslaw and cardboard biscuit. AAA will assure him of his accommodations when he grows weary of "camping"; his Visa and MasterCard are everywhere accepted; and uniform shopping malls, a supermarket at one end and a liquor store at the other, reduce the possibility of disorientation. It's almost like staying home.

Until 1979, when the paved highway was completed to Port Hardy, the northern third of Vancouver Island was spared the tourist assault. The "Ho Chi Minh Trail," as Bill Mackay refers to the preasphalt road, was a serious proposition, an axle buster, a muffler masher that discouraged frivolous expeditions. True, the heaviest concentration of out-of-province visitors still occurs south of Campbell River, but that may be changing—as the great increase in tourist traffic to Telegraph Cove suggests.

In the early 1920s Fred Westell came upon this little inlet, no more than a hundred yards wide and a few hundred yards long, realized its potential as a small harbor, and bought it. He built a steam-powered sawmill at one end and a heavy plank boardwalk to support a handful of tiny cottages and a few storage buildings; he allowed a number of Japanese fishermen to live in the houses. When World War Two broke out, the Canadian military commandeered the whole shebang, removed the Japanese (whose countrymen had, for unfathomable reasons, shelled the remote and strategically useless lighthouse at Estevan Point below Nootka Sound), and used Westell's facility to process sitka spruce for Mosquito fighter planes. When the war was over they returned everything to him, rebuilt and improved as they had promised, and the remote little backwater continued undisturbed for another thirty-five years.

Which is how I first saw it in 1981. Coming down the rutted road from Beaver Cove I pulled into an empty parking lot, muddy and flecked with rain puddles, and sat wondering if the place was inhabited. The floating docks contained a skiff or two, a purse-seiner tied up for the night (the week? the month?), an old freight hauler that looked as if it were seldom used. The sawmill was silent, though a raft of logs floated in the pen. There seemed nothing alive except a solitary raven amusing himself by doing barrel rolls over the mouth of the cove. Eventually two old geezers came walking down the boardwalk; we chatted a few moments, and they opined that I could probably camp at the end

Morning fog over White Cliffs, off Vancouver Island.

Telegraph Cove, Vancouver Island.

of a logging road that ran up into the trees behind the mill. Which I did. Without human companionship. In a no-see-um rookery.

Things were a bit different in 1984. The parking lot was jammed with cars, pickups, motor homes, vans. Kayaks were piled like cordwood along the quay; there was an hour-long line at the haul-out ramp; and the road to the rookery was lined for a half-mile with boat trailers. My inquiry at a new mobile "office" about the prospects of camping produced only amusement from the lady behind the counter. "We've been booked solid since the first of June," she said.

Booked? An official campground? Toilets? Showers? Hook-ups? "The last time I was here," I said, "you could have bivouacked a battalion up there in that clearing."

"There *is* a battalion in that clearing," she said. "Best salmon fishing around, right out in the straits. Now the road's good, the word's out."

Sunflower star, Donegal Head, Malcolm Island.

The best salmon fishing around isn't so good this year, however, at least according to Jim Borrowman—and not because the road is in and the word is out. We sit in the *Gukumi*'s galley drinking coffee and watching Frans Lanting and Bill Mackay marshal the troops ashore in the herring tender so they can explore and record an intertidal zone uncovered by an exceptionally low tide. The rain begins to fall harder, though the temperature is pleasantly mild. "There have just been fewer fish," Jim says, "maybe something to do with the natural cycle, maybe not. Greed wiped out the herring fishery up here four years ago when the Japanese began paying $3,500 a ton for fish that had a local market value of maybe up to $180 a ton. I don't suppose salmon are exempt from exploitation."

Indeed, nobody knows precisely why the catch is down, or whether things will get better or worse, but if the history of "resource harvesting" in other areas is any indication, it is not difficult to speculate. It will get worse. Part of the problem is that no particular interest group is willing to assume any measure of responsibility. The gill-netters blame the purse-seiners, and the purse-seiners blame the gill-netters; commercial fishermen blame sport fishermen, and vice versa; fishery personnel blame logging practices, and the loggers speak only to God. The provincial government is, of course, concerned, and supports the fisheries program, and yet it cannot deny itself the revenue and so leases every twig on the island. It also comes up with ideas like the "buy back" program. Concluding that the real problem lies in the size of the fishing fleet, it proposes to pay fishermen twice the value of their crummy old boats in order to eliminate them from service. Many old salts, however, observe that this is an opportunity to plow the profit back into a bigger, faster, better-equipped vessel. The end result may be a reduced fleet, but one with five times the capabilities of the old—one that can now fish all year round and in any kind of weather. "Where does this end?" Borrowman wonders. "When we're down to four boats and three fish?"

Poor fishing, it must be observed, is a relative term off Vancouver Island. Chinook in the spring, then the coho, and in late summer the sockeye and pink salmon run. Five species are indigenous to the coastal waters of British Columbia, but the Chinook (also known as the Alaska king salmon) is the game fish of choice among sport fishermen. Chinooks live longer than any of the others, up to seven years, and can attain a weight of over 100 pounds. By contrast, pinks are the smallest Pacific species, living only two years and generally reaching a maximum weight of only four to five pounds.

The tidal waters are also rich in rockfish, flounder, sole, and halibut, as well as a variety of shellfish; Borrowman, to kill time while we wait for the photographers, puts on his wetsuit and tank and goes down to explore the possibilities beneath a kelp bed off our stern. I watch his bubbles for a time; then a minke whale blows just a few hundred yards out in the sound, and my attention is diverted. The minke is a small baleen whale about 25 feet in length that feeds on plankton, straining its meal through a wall of bristly

Bald eagle stooping for herring, Baronet Passage.

Gwayasdums village on Gilford Island, 1900.
Courtesy British Columbia Provincial Museum.

slats growing from his upper jaw. A rorqual whale (the family *Balaenopteridae*), in some measure it resembles the greatest leviathan, the blue, and is, in fact, named for a Norwegian whaler who somehow managed to confuse the two beasts. Mr. Minke was drunk, no doubt. It's hard to imagine how he could mistake one of the smallest of the Cetacea for the largest creature that has ever lived on this planet.

Borrowman returns with three black abalone, a couple of scallops, and a sea cucumber. The sea cucumber has nothing to do with subtidal flora, as its name suggests. It does not, as its name suggests, resemble anything cool and crispy resting atop a chef's salad. Lying in a pail with its innards removed, it looks like something one might find surrounded by crows in the middle of the road, but filet out its long, thin strips of meat, fry it in a little oil and garlic, and it tastes better than abalone. Can be passed off as abalone too, which it will be tonight when it makes its debut on the hors d'oeuvres plate. Borrowman seems a bit guilty about the abs and the scallops. "Truth is I hardly go down for food

Kwakiutl animal masks, Gilford Island.

Nootka whaler with bearskin and sealskin floats.
Courtesy British Columbia Provincial Museum.

anymore," he says. "Overharvesting has really depleted the shellfish, just like everything else. I don't even tell my diving buddies anymore when I come across a good reef because they'll pick it clean in a week."

The conversation on the *Gikumi* seems frequently to run to the misuse, overuse, and depletion of the island's natural resources, and much of the abuse has a familiarly local focus. The worst offenders are often the old-timers, native sons, and permanent residents who see resource reduction as the result of foreign pressure and are damned if they're going to support controls that might include themselves among the controlled. "Hunting up here on the northern end of the island is a good case in point," Bill Mackay remarks on the way back to Telegraph Cove. "Getting here used to take a big effort, but those who did could drive down a logging road and shoot a deer right from the cab. With the road paved, hunting quadrupled, and with all that increased pressure it meant that people pretty soon had to actually get out of their cars and walk into the woods if they wanted any venison. There are some pretty lazy hunters around, you know, and it makes them mad. Deer are getting so scarce you have to go looking for them. It never occurs to anybody that this 'problem' stems from too many hunters," Mackay says. "To them it's *wolves*. Too many wolves. So now everybody's out killing wolves . . . they shot over a hundred last year in the Nimpkish Valley alone."

Well, it's not an original idea. If you can't blame the government, or out-of-staters, blame the wolves.

I t is unfair to people like Bill Mackay and Jim Borrowman to imply that all Canadians are indifferent to wilderness management and wildlife protection. Far from it. The wretched example set below the 49th parallel has not been lost on a great many people scattered throughout the Northwest islands, and a number of them, even those who get a little shifty-eyed when labeled environmentalists, are taking an activist stand against those who see nature as an expendable resource off which to make a quick buck. On Vancouver Island, where so many are dependent on the lumber industry for their livelihood, the voice of controlled development and protectionism can find itself rather friendless in a crowd. But it can be heard—as it was during the recent fight to save Robson Bight.

Robson Bight doesn't even show on the Complete Map of Vancouver Island, but to whale-watching freaks it is the newest hot spot, a fledgling Scammon's Lagoon, even if accessible to most only through the pages of the *National Geographic* and an occasional American television outdoor adventure series. For Robson Bight, a shallow cove along the northeast coast and just a few miles south of Alert Bay, is the playpen of the resident

Black bear, northern Vancouver Island.

pods of killer whales whose range includes the Inside Passage. The beaches along the cove are composed of smooth, black rocks about the size of golf balls, and for reasons that are largely conjectural *Orcinus orca* takes great delight in rubbing its body over these stones in the shallow tide zone. ("Great delight" is also conjecture, though it seems a reasonable assumption to anyone watching this behavior.)

But the battle to save these rubbing beaches had little to do initially with orcas, or for that matter with the rubbing beaches. The Tsitika River empties into the Johnstone Strait at Robson Bight, draining nearly 100,000 acres of watershed around the Franklin Range and Derby Mountain. The area is extremely precipitous, the slopes of the Tsitika River canyon rising over a mile in places, and it remains, partly because of its ruggedness and partly because a moratorium on timber cutting was placed on it during the early 1970s, the only unlogged watershed on the island. A change in government, however, resulted in the moratorium being lifted and the preparation of an "integrated resource plan" that would allow logging while "protecting" valuable Dolly Varden and steelhead spawning habitat.

The protective language might as well have included phrases like "we hope" and "if at all possible" and "so long as the economic interests of MacMillan–Bloedel are not impacted." Skeptics including Jim and Anne Borrowman, Bill and Donna Mackay, and a marine biologist named Bill Harrower felt that logging the Tsitika wilderness would inevitably lead to siltation, erosion, destruction of riparian habitat as well as water quality—in short, the degradation of the entire watershed. In response, they formed the Robson Bight Preservation Committee, prepared and presented an environmental report on the dangers of development, and were ignored. MacMillan–Bloedel went ahead with plans to bulldoze the estuary and build a dry-land sort—a place to grade, scale, and separate types of logs before dumping them in the bight to be floated down to the mills at Campbell River. They also planned to log the tidewater area.

Decision time. The founders of the preservation committee knew very well about the rubbing beaches and the killer whales who frequented them during late summer. They also knew that in spite of a certain local indifference to orcas, generally regarded as salmon-eating nuisances and referred to as "fat choppers" and "blackfish," there was a whole world of whale lovers out there whose energies could be tapped in opposition to the timber companies. This too had its drawbacks. Whale watching as a spectator sport currently being one of the most popular manifestations of loving nature to death, publicity about the orcas would put Robson Bight on the wilderness-experience map. The prospect of a cove filled with logs became the prospect of a cove filled with people. But the alternative was no cove at all, and the whales were brought in as an issue in the campaign.

"We had posters made," Jim Borrowman recalls. "We stumped up and down the island giving film presentations and talks, we circulated petitions, we took a bunch of

Kwakiutl elders gathered for raising of totem pole,
Watson Island.

Detail of Kwakiutl totem pole,
Alert Bay, Malcolm Island.

media people down to the bight on the *Gikumi* and right away every paper in Canada was running the story." Under such pressure the provincial government established a task force to review the facts and figures, and in the end Robson Bight was declared an ecological preserve and the rubbing beaches off-limits when the whales were in occupancy, and whale watchers were required to maintain a 300-meter distance from the animals. The MacMillan–Bloedel dry-land sort and log dump had been defeated.

One might not go so far as to call this a pyrrhic victory, but success was certainly not without cost. As the Mackays and Borrowmans predicted, the teeming hordes descended—in kayaks, in powerboats, in rubber dinghies, in canoes; with sails, motors, and oars. Some even felt compelled to don wetsuits and leap in the water—a kind of swim-with-Namu number that was not exactly in keeping with the spirit of an ecological preserve. But "spirit" was all the provincial government invested in its decree. When they are in the area Mackay and Borrowman have accepted (a little reluctantly) the role of volunteer wardens; but they have no authority to remove or cite people for violating the restrictions, and neither seems to relish the role of policeman. About all they can do is tell people about the reserve when they find them in violation of the rules, and hope the spirit moves them to maintain the 300-meter distance and refrain from camping on the beach.

And the Tsitika River valley will still be logged. MacMillan–Bloedel will have to locate its dump farther south, at the mouth of the Eve River, or haul its timber inland along roads it will gouge out of the mountainside. But the steep slopes will be clearcut, erosion will ruin the fish habitat, MOW (material other than water) will undoubtedly begin to flow into the estuary at Robson Bight. "How this will affect the whales," says Borrowman, "is anybody's guess."

The alarm on my watch goes off an hour early. Instead of smashing it with the hatchet as it richly deserves, I crawl out of the tent and pull on my boots. The Forest Service campground that I found after dark is empty, and I feel a somber sense of aloneness as I stand contemplating the damp, vaporous breaths that drift through the banks of vegetation around me. The path down to the Nimpkish River where I go to splash my face is hacked through a jungle of salmonberry, and the banks above the stream are thickly fringed by alder. A blue heron stands in the quiet waters of a back eddy on the opposite shore, and I can hear a pileated woodpecker hammering in the trees from which I have just emerged.

Stepping out on some exposed rocks to make my ablutions, I startle a blacktail deer drinking from the edge of a gravel bar a few hundred feet downstream. She raises her

Hemlock and maple at forest edge,
Cathedral Grove, Vancouver Island.

Bald eagle killed by gunshot, near
Desolation Sound.

Loggers putting undercut in red cedar,
circa 1924. Courtesy Provincial Archives
of British Columbia.

head swiftly from the river, glances wildly at me for a second, then bounds across the shallows and into the brush. Her panic triggers memory. Three years ago, lost in a tangled mass of salal near an inlet east of Telegraph Cove, I finally clawed my way to an old cedar tree and climbed up in it to get my bearings. Trying to get a vantage from a patch of salal had been like trying to walk on water, but the cedar showed me the cove was only a stone's throw away and easily accessible along a creekbed to my right. It also showed me what my ears had for some moments been recording—the noise of something crashing through the forest as if in flight, and not too particular about what was in the way. A blacktail doe pursued by a cougar flashed beneath my tree. Tongue out, flanks heaving, she cleared a patch of thimbleberry, took the cobble beach in two extraordinary leaps, and hit the water of the inlet with her legs churning so furiously she left a wake. The cougar vanished. For ten minutes I watched the doe swim straight out into the sound, until I could no longer see her in the light chop on the water.

Back in camp I search for dry wood to boil some coffee, but after I clamber over the fifth rotten log with hemlock seedlings growing in its humus, find nothing but banana slugs, moss, bracken fern, and fungus, the message gets in. There *is* no dry wood on northern Vancouver Island. Dry and northern Vancouver Island are a contradiction in terms. No matter. There will be coffee on the *Gikumi* when I get back to Telegraph Cove. And with luck, and in spite of my sanctimonious mutterings about whale watchers and the craze for adventures-in-nature, there will be orcas in Robson Bight today. It's just for the photographers. The photographers make us do these things.

Orcinus orca, unlike many other cetacean species once numerous in the northern Pacific (the grey, the humpback, the fin, the right), was never hunted to near extinction. Why bother with a 25-foot orca when greys and rights came twice as long, and fins up to 75 and 80 feet? But these undersized creatures, the current darlings of everybody's marineland sideshow, were hardly excused from persecution. At the local level fishermen shot them whenever opportunity presented because of their piggish appetite for salmon. On a more global scale the U.S. Air Force found them useful as targets for fighter pilots who needed strafing practice; the U.S. Navy machinegunned and depth-charged them by the hundreds in the north Atlantic to appease Icelandic fishermen who objected to their competition for fish; the Russians were curious about the contents of their stomachs and cut open nearly 1,000 of them to have a looksee. What they saw was everything from pieces of other whales to pinnipeds to sea turtles. And the subjects, of course, paid rather heavily for this contribution to knowledge.

Fascination with killer whale behavior did not really become widespread until the famous Namu was captured in 1965 off Vancouver Island—though Kenneth Norris at the University of California, Santa Cruz, had begun studying their vocalizations much earlier. By the 1970s researchers from all over had gotten in on the act, and by 1984

Whale watchers, Johnstone Strait.

probably more was known about *Orcinus orca* (particularly those in the Pacific Northwest) than any other whale in the sea. For one thing, they survive in captivity and can be studied close hand; for another, the communities that range off the British Columbia and Washington coasts stay within a limited area and can be easily monitored.

One of these researchers, John Ford, a young marine biologist from the University of British Columbia, pulls alongside the *Gikumi* as we cruise south along the Johnstone Strait, and ties his motorboat to the herring tender. It is raining again (naturally), and the prospect of hot chicken soup and salmon sandwiches probably impells him as much as the prospect of explaining four years of orca research to the soggy crowd in the galley. But he seems cheerfully willing to do so (for the five-hundredth time?) and has even brought along some tapes to illustrate what he has to say about whale "language."

The killer whale, as John Cunningham Lilly observed in his 1961 book, *Man and Dolphin,* has a brain four times the size of man's, and much of it is cerebral cortex—the part that handles, among other things, language. It was very likely, Lilly postulated, that whales had a highly sophisticated system of communication, and he suggested some experiments that might prove his thesis. Some scientists felt that he demonstrated himself one brick short of a load when he proposed rigging a telephone connection between a whale in captivity and its folks back home, but John Ford's research has gone a long way toward suggesting that Lilly's idea was not so utterly absurd as it initially sounded.

Two distinct communities of killer whales inhabit the waters of the Inside Passage: one that ranges around the Gulf and San Juan Islands, another that stays in the Johnstone and Queen Charlotte straits. Within each community are subgroups called pods (twelve in the northern configuration, three in the southern), and evidence from both sightings and sound recordings indicate that these pods swim, feed, and rest as a unit. Individuals within a pod are distinguishable by peculiarities of the dorsal fin (a kind of orca thumb print), but also by the distinct "language" they speak. The pattern of squeaks, clicks, shrills, squeals, and other ham-radio yowls is identical among the members of a given pod; it is completely unlike the pattern in any other pod. From listening to vocalization patterns, in short, Ford can tell which pod an animal comes from. He can tell, for example, where the celebrated Namu comes from.

All of the information that Ford has recorded (he has been observed in Telegraph Cove sleeping next to speakers wired to hydrophones out in the strait) has added greatly not only to information about vocalizations but about orca social behavior as well—a structure that suggests a closely knit, matriarchal family unit in which an old cow (who may live as long as one hundred years) travels in consort with her offspring, male and female. Therefore, since it is possible to identify the pod from which Namu was taken, it is also possible to identify Namu's mother. *John Ford knows Namu's mother.* Let's rig up a telephone and see if they'll have a conversation.

Seastack and fishing boat, Barkley Sound, Vancouver Island.

Nootka man and woman, 1778.
Courtesy Bancroft Library.

Let's at least drop a hydrophone in the water and see if she's in for a rub this afternoon. But the more spectacular orca show at Robson Bight is not on today. No leaping, breaching, spy-hopping (raising their heads vertically above the surface)—just a dozen or so passersby having a short massage, then cruising down the strait in the direction of Kelsey Bay. The photographers bang away with telephoto lenses the size of rocket launchers as Frans, who has spent much of last month taking pictures of humpbacks up along the coast of Alaska, looks on indifferently from behind his twenty-third salmon sandwich. Watching the whale watchers is not nearly as interesting as watching whales, but today it will have to do.

What is intriguing, however, is the conflict of interest that shows up in conversation with Jim Borrowman and Bill Mackay while the whales are in the bight and the cameras click. They are stuck with an unresolvable dilemma—even for two people whose intelligent concern for the environment transcends their use and enjoyment of its undeveloped space. Whale-watching tours aren't exactly how they most wish to utilize the *Gikumi,* but they have to eat. Their families have to eat. It costs money to run and maintain a boat, and it can't be made just by hauling freight to hand-loggers up in the British Columbia fiords, or by taking people scuba diving. The whale-watching trips help pay the bills. At the same time they contribute to the problem of overexposure by man and his machinery in a marine reserve. They assist in the process of regulation; they are a part of the intrusion that needs regulating. It is something of a paradox, Borrowman admits. "And it's the same with hauling freight. I take up parts and equipment so the loggers can go on clearcutting the damn forest. If you want to live up here you often find yourself assisting the very things you oppose."

So it is with the whale-watching tours. The fight to save Robson Bight, led by Borrowman and Mackay, was to protect a watershed and to preserve important habitat for whales, not to protect a place for people to go and *watch* whales. It is enough that we capture them and put them in oceanariums and teach them to jump through hoops for a piece of herring. And whether one is talking about orcas or eagles or deer or Dolly Varden, the only possibility for salvation over the long run is a serious acceptance of both the connotative and denotative meaning of such classifications as "marine sanctuary" and "ecological reserve." Reserved for whom? we need to ask. A place of refuge for whom? And from what?

EPILOGUE
THE VIEW AHEAD

Man has too long forgotten that the earth was
given to him for usufruct alone, not for
consumption, still less for profligate waste.

George Perkins Marsh

The boat is loaded with the last of the personal belongings. The lightkeeper's wife and child have already been ferried to the mainland; the lightkeeper himself makes one last pass over his domain before returning it to wind and weather. He checks the locks on the foghorn building and blockhouse, secures the cistern cover, adjusts the clamps on a metal shutter. On his way down to the haul-out where the assistant is waiting, he stops at the hutch where two rabbits, pets his daughter will soon remember and whose absence he will try to explain, munch on the remains of the vegetables his wife cleaned out of the icebox before she closed the house. For a moment he considers his options, then lets the door of the cage swing open and walks on down to the beach.

A disastrous cycle has begun. In a year these two harmless hares will become twenty-two; in three years, 222. They will feed on the fragile vegetation covering the higher parts of the island, procreate, multiply, and divide. The vegetation will become more and more sparse, unable to keep up with the overgrazing to which it is subjected. The white-crowned sparrow and killdeer who have always nested in its protective cover will find it increasingly difficult to find adequate shelter in which to raise their young. Their numbers will dwindle, and then they will abandon the island altogether. The rabbits, however, having no natural predators other than their own appetites, will go on munching, multiplying, and dividing.

Eventually the vegetation will become so thin it will no longer hold the soil, and erosion will unnaturally accelerate. Wind will move the sand toward the ledges, blow it in great sheets into the tidal surge. Winter storms will gully the sedimentary beds now exposed, and begin to carry loosened rocks and pebbles down toward the sea. The island is shrinking, crumbling, blowing into the current. In twenty years it will serve someone's environmental studies class as a fine example of the interrelated processes that sustain an ecosystem and of the consequences that result from inadvertent tampering.

There is seldom much one can do about inadvertent tampering until after the fact. The lightkeeper's actions were perhaps ill-considered, but they were not *un*considered or inhumane. He was doing his daughter's bunnies a favor. He had no information on which to base an understanding of the long-term effects. The point is not to become so biocentric in one's concern for nature that one wishes to eliminate the influence of human occupancy from the planet—an objective that is impossible even if some might think it desirable. But we can learn from our mistakes, we can moderate our impact, we can on occasion even repair some of our blunders. We have, in fact, begun doing so.

The abuse to which most of our coastal islands have been subjected can never be reversed—indeed, in the Pacific Northwest, abuse is still only diffidently understood by most inhabitants—but at such places as the Farallons, Año Nuevo, and the Channel Islands, a great deal has been done in recent years to protect the existing environment from further degradation and to begin restoring it to a closer approximation of its indigenous state. Some endemic flora have been reintroduced; some exotic fauna such as rabbits, goats, and rats have been reduced in numbers or eliminated altogether; human intrusion has been curtailed by the establishment of marine sanctuaries, state reserves, and a national park. In short, we *do* understand a great deal more about relationships within ecosystems, and we *have* made a little progress toward reducing the impact of our overwhelming presence. Unfortunately, we are successful only when the political and economic implications of restraints and regulations are minimized.

And there are certainly no permanent guarantees, even when protective custody resides in the hands of what ought to be (but isn't) the agency least susceptible to special interest pressure—the federal government. It is no secret that the Reagan administration policy toward the environment, onshore and offshore, has been to exploit it for material benefit—explore it, develop it, lease it to political cronies, drill it, cut it, mine it. True, former Secretary of the Interior James Watt so alarmed the American people with his

Page 124: Echachis Island and Clayoquot Sound, Vancouver Island.

Sea otter, California coast.

frenzied intention to give away most of the public domain in one short term of office that he undermined himself at almost every major bend in the road. But the policies he pursued did not noticeably change when Mr. Watt, tired perhaps of merely hoisting himself, took his petard out on the plain and fell upon it. The policies were simply invested in a quieter spokesman, William P. Clark, holder of the worst environmental record of any judge to serve on the California Supreme Court.

For the moment Mr. Clark seems to be following a conciliatory, low-profile role, particularly in respect to outer continental shelf lease sales and the oceans, beaches, and coastal areas that would be impacted by oil exploration. There has not been much talk lately about reversing the protected status of the waters around the Channel Islands and allowing drilling to take place within the marine sanctuary. Clark has delayed two lease sales and insists he will not consider others until there is a programmatic balance between environmental protection and development. Not everyone is convinced. Cynics point out that the oil companies haven't yet explored most of the tracts they already possess, and there is clearly no need to hastily reactivate the antagonisms of the Watt years.

If the furor over oil lease sales has temporarily calmed down, mineral-right lease sales have yet to attract the public's attention. But major concerns in this area must be addressed. "It is the policy of this administration," Mr. Reagan said shortly after his election in 1980, "to decrease America's minerals vulnerability." And two years later the United States voted against an International Law of the Sea Treaty that had been delicately negotiated over a period of ten years because, as Mr. Reagan said, "the deep seabed mining part of the convention does not meet U.S. objectives." Shortly thereafter he declared all mineral resources within 200 miles off America's coasts to be contained within an "exclusive economic zone" belonging to the United States, and he directed the Department of the Interior to study its potential for development.

The reason behind all this interest was the discovery in 1977 of hydrothermal vent systems on the ocean floor that produce deposits of polymetallic sulfides (zinc-copper-iron-sulfur compounds with trace amounts of various metals such as gold, silver, chromium, manganese, aluminum, and so on). The technology to conduct submarine mining is undeveloped; there is no evidence that polymetallics contain sufficient strategic minerals to justify tearing up the sea floor; and there is no information about the environmental consequences to the benthic terrain, to plankton and fish larvae, indeed to anything in the marine food chain that might be affected by the disruption such an operation implies. Nevertheless, in March of 1983 the Department of the Interior announced its intention to lease an undersea canyon called the Gorda Ridge 150 miles off the coast of California and Oregon. It may be a long time before it is mined, but when it is, the effect on the Pacific Northwest fishery may be severe—and may, in turn, affect the seabirds and marine mammals that depend on the fishery.

And while it is comforting to read that the U.S. Navy has decided not to scuttle nine nuclear submarines (complete with their radioactive engine compartments) at various deep-sea disposal sites, the fact that it was even proposed forces one to consider the possibility that in the long run the destruction to our coastal environment caused by our whaler, sealer, and egger forebears may appear minor in comparison to the effects of oil and mineral exploration and the use of our oceans as repositories for industrial, municipal, and nuclear waste. Gregory Bateson once remarked that if we insist on seeing ourselves as *outside* of everything around us, and attach neither moral nor ethical considerations to our world, then our surroundings seem to us there simply for purposes of exploitation. "If this is your estimate of your relation to nature *and you have an advanced technology,"* he admonishes, "you will die either of the toxic by-product of your own hate, or, simply, of overpopulation and overgrazing. The raw materials of the world are finite."

As the lightkeeper's bunnies discovered.

The Landsat photograph of North America continues to hang on my studio wall, and the long, sweeping line of unbroken coast from Baja to Cape Flattery hasn't changed

Tlingit totem pole, Revillagigedo Island.

Pulp mill near Campbell River, Vancouver Island.

Humpback whale diving, southeast Alaska.

since I first began looking at it—same blip off the Point Reyes peninsula, same smudges in the Santa Barbara and San Pedro channels, same bark on the fishhook bay at Scammon's Lagoon. Landsat is certainly evidence of an advanced technology. And it is certainly an "outside" view of the world that attaches no moral significance to what it reveals. But it is only a machine. And it doesn't offer an image of the earth that any, save a few astronauts, are likely to see. The arid slopes of Cedros, the enshrouded cliffs of the Channel Islands, the narrow beaches and granitic shelves of Año Nuevo and the Farallons, the serpentine waterways and densely forested islands of the Inside Passage—all are witnessed by most of us from the platform of our own shoes, and with growing awareness that we are anything but ecologically detached from our surroundings. There are inconsistencies in our environmental ethic, to be sure, but there is also a greater community of effort toward the preservation of our remaining wilderness than ever before. As the incumbent planetary custodians there is some reason to believe that we are slowly becoming as concerned with putting things back together as we have been skillful at taking them apart.

Island in fog, Queen Charlotte Strait.

PHOTOGRAPHER'S NOTES
by Frans Lanting

MORE PEOPLE HELPED in more ways with providing access to places and information than I can acknowledge here. Those not mentioned may find solace in the fact that not every island on the West Coast has found its way into this book either.

I would like to thank Dr. Burney LeBoeuf and his co-workers at the University of California at Santa Cruz, in particular Rick Condit, Bob Gisiner, and Marianne Riedman, for helping to make fieldwork at Año Nuevo Island possible.

The United States Fish and Wildlife Service provided access to the Farallon Islands, the Oceanic Society and the Coast Guard got me out and back; and Bob Boekelheide, Teya McElroy, and Larry Spear of the Point Reyes Bird Observatory helped me to understand the place and its inhabitants.

I owe thanks to William Ehorn and Nick Whelan of the National Park Service, who facilitated my fieldwork in the Channel Islands, as did Russ and Scott Philbrick. Doug DeMaster of the National Marine Fisheries Service, Brent Stewart of Hubbs Seaworld, and Frank Gress of the University of California at Davis took me along on research trips to Anacapa and San Miguel Island.

Jesus Castro, Jorge Medina, and José Sanchez Rodriguez were gracious hosts at Cabo Norte on Isla Cedros, where the going would have been tougher without Larry Minden.

Gregg Blomberg and Geremy Snapp put me up and brought me down to the slow pace of Lopez Island in the San Juans.

I have many friends to thank for hosting and helping me get around the islands of British Columbia: Bill and Donna Mackay along with Jim and Ann Borrowman of Telegraph Cove, Graeme and Linda Ellis of Nanaimo, Debbie and John Ford and Ulli Steltzer of Vancouver, and Joe David of Tofino. Elsie Williams of the Kwawaineuk band in Hee-Ghums (Hopetown) and Alice and Fred Smith as well as Sam "Cougar" Johnson of the Kwicksutaineuk band in Gwayasdums honored me with their hospitality and allowed me to document their way of life, which Peter Macnair of the British Columbia Provincial Museum helped to interpret.

Roger Luckenbach deserves special mention for educating a newcomer to the West Coast to many facets of its natural and social history.

Last but not least I want to express my gratitude to the wild creatures depicted in this book. Sanderling, elephant seal, and all their kin along the coast opened my eyes to a new world, and their portraits helped to pay the rent while I was learning.

The notes that follow provide more extensive background information on the illustrations in this book—both my own photographs and the historical illustrations—than brief captions can accommodate. I am grateful to all the institutions who granted permission to reproduce historical material.

INTRODUCTION: The View from Above

PAGE II: One of hundreds of islets off Vancouver Island that are unnamed on official maps.

PAGE VIII: A long exposure turns breaking surf into mist in this evening scene at Año Nuevo Island.

PAGE 3:   Few outsiders ever have a chance to walk on the wild shores of Santa Rosa Island. Its private owners bar all but official visitors from this island off Santa Barbara.

A western gull (*Larus occidentalis*) incubating a clutch of three eggs amidst blooming sea-fig. Breeding gulls develop a red spot on their lower mandibles, which their young will instinctively peck at to elicit feeding.

PAGE 5:   Bunchberry is a typical understory plant of the Northwestern forests. It relies for seed dispersal on animals that eat the brightly colored berries that stand out amidst the somber tones of the forest floor.

PAGE 7:   By 1602, when this map was drawn, many prominent features of the California coast were already known to Sebastián Vizcaíno and other explorers who headed north from Spanish strongholds in Mexico. *Courtesy Bancroft Library.*

PAGE 8:   This young elephant seal has survived great white sharks and many other rigors during its first year in the open ocean. Not much is known about the life of elephant seals at sea, for despite a West Coast population now exceeding 100,000 individuals, they are seldom seen offshore. However, recent experiments by Dr. Burney LeBoeuf and his associates indicate that *Mirounga angustirostris* is a superb diver capable of staying under water for a half-hour and reaching depths of several hundred meters.

PAGE 11:   Low morning clouds part just enough to guide the pilot of the float plane from which this picture was taken. The roadless British Columbia coast relies heavily on air taxis for transport between remote settlements and the outside world.

PAGE 12:   In fading twilight a brown pelican (*Pelecanus occidentalis*) hovers momentarily before plunging to feed on a school of anchovy.

ON THE WATERFRONT: Isla Cedros, Baja

PAGE 14:   Like most of the Baja coast, the shores of Isla Cedros are rugged and uninhabited. Along most of its east side, mountains plunge down to the ocean; access to the interior is only possible through narrow canyons.

PAGE 19:   The shamans of precolonial Cedros forbade their people under threat of illness or death to look towards the Islas San Benitos, three islands that lie seventeen miles off Cedros. There is no conclusive archeological evidence that any native people ever inhabited the Benitos. Although today there is a small fishing village, people are still far outnumbered by pinnipeds.

PAGE 21:   The vegetation on Cedros reflects that of the nearby Baja desert. Sparse in many parts of the island, it becomes lusher in dry streambeds, where agave and elephant tree can soak up water during rare rainstorms.

PAGE 23:   The cedars for which Cedros was named, by Captain Francisco de Ulloa in 1540, are actually junipers (*Juniperus californica*). They live only on the island's highest hills, which are cooler and receive more moisture than the lowlands. Within a stone's throw of the junipers one may encounter palms, cacti, and lichens as well.

The cannery and the salt-loading operations provide badly needed income for Cedros residents and permit the importation of a few consumer goods from Ensenada. John Lennon's "Greatest Hits" can be found at the island's only record shop, but during medical calamities the island's isolation is suddenly very real.

PAGES 24–25:   One of the earliest known views of Isla Cedros is a delicate watercolor painting by George Sykes here reproduced in black-and-white. Sykes was an artist aboard George Vancouver's sloop *Discovery* during a journey that lasted from 1791 to 1795. *Courtesy Bancroft Library.*

PAGES 26 and 32:   The shantytown appearance of small villages along the Baja coast reflects a low material standard of living but not the high degree of hospitality upheld by many of their inhabitants. Many fishermen on Cedros and elsewhere are organized in fishing co-ops, which provide low-cost loans for boats and guarantee the purchase of their members' catch.

PAGE 27:   Grim-looking and impenetrable to humans, patches of opuntia cactus are essential habitat for creatures such as small rodents, which find nourishment in the cactus pads, and cactus wrens, which build safe nesting sites between the spines.

PAGE 29:   Blooming signals the end of a long life for the agave, also known as century plant, which dies shortly after sending a massive flowering stalk up from a ground-hugging rosette.

PAGE 31:   The sand dollar skeletons found on sandy beaches give little information about the living creatures they represent. Sand dollars may live for up to thirteen years, spending their lives partially buried on sandy sea bottoms. They form colonies whose density sometimes exceeds 600 individuals per square meter, and employ tube feet to gather food. The species depicted here (*Encope micropora*) occurs from southern California to Peru.

Whether nesting or feeding, western gulls are never far from the ocean, unlike some other gulls that make their homes in the Great Basin or in prairie potholes. Western gulls dominate coastal bird communities from Baja up to Washington, where the closely related glaucous-winged gull (*Larus glaucescens*) takes over its niche.

The distribution of the California sea lion (*Zalophus californianus*) parallels that of the western gull, but extends a little farther into the coastal waters of British Columbia. In the northern half of their range they coexist with the larger northern or Steller's sea lion.

PAGE 33:   The elephant tree (*Pachycormus discolor*) displays adaptations found in many desert-dwelling plants. It reduces evaporation by minimizing leaf surface area, and during dry periods it sheds its leaves altogether and stores vital nutrients within its contorted trunk.

PAGE 34:   Tour boats carrying North American tourists to the calving grounds of grey whales in Laguna San Ignacio (Scammon's Lagoon) often stop at the Islas San Benitos or Cedros to trade beer and T-shirts for lobster with local fishermen.

AMERICAN GALAPAGOS: The Channel Islands

PAGE 36:   Point Bennett, situated at the western tip of San Miguel Island, near the edge of the continental shelf, is one of the great wildlife sanctuaries of the West Coast. Many thousands of seals and sea lions representing six species haul out on its gently sloping beaches to rest after fishing forays along the edge of the continental shelf.

PAGE 39:   According to the Santa Barbara *Weekly Herald* of September 5, 1889, this photograph depicts a "party of hardy adventurers, organized by some of our local scientists, who were in search of needed rest and recreation, which they proposed to accomplish by exploring the islands of the eastern end of the Channel for the purpose of examining into the Natural History." Some artists were invited along "so that we might be able to bring with us on our return, photographs and sketches of interest and in this manner share our pleasure with those who had not the good fortune to be with us." *Courtesy Bancroft Library.*

PAGE 41:   The three islands of Anacapa Island—West, Middle, and East Anacapa—are actually one landform with submerged connections. Only East Anacapa is accessible to the public; the National Park Service maintains a small campground there.

PAGE 42:   In spring and summer Anacapa Island hosts the only West Coast breeding colony of brown pelicans within U.S. boundaries. In the early 1970's DDT poisoning caused a near-total collapse of the colony, which is now in the process of recovery.

PAGE 43:   Most sanderlings (*Calidris alba*) on the West Coast are migrants quickly passing on their way to distant wintering grounds in South America or scattered nesting sites in the high Arctic. Some linger all winter, however. They briefly interrupt their frenzied lifestyle along the tideline to doze in small flocks during high tide.

PAGE 45: The tree sunflower, or giant coreopsis (*Coreopsis gigantea*), occurs outside the Channel Islands, but nowhere in the same spectacular density it reaches in this archipelago. Some people claim they can see its yellow blaze on Anacapa Island from the mainland twenty-four miles away.

PAGE 47: Among male elephant seals, confrontations are primarily a game of bluff. A shrewd, experienced bull can drive off many opponents with the right combination of mean looks and deep, gutteral roars. Battles are usually decided with one or two heavy blows and rarely lead to the extended bloodshed shown here.

PAGE 48: For over a decade Herbert Lester and his family, here shown displaying their distress-signal flag, were the sole human inhabitants of San Miguel Island. *Courtesy McNally & Loftin, Publishers, Santa Barbara.*

PAGE 49: The seastacks off the eastern tip of Anacapa are one of the landmarks of Channel Islands National Park.

PAGE 50: Undoing the damage inflicted by livestock upon the native vegetation of the Channel Islands is one of the main tasks of conservationists.

PAGE 52: William Ehorn, the current superintendent of Channel Islands National Park, holds a brown pelican chick during a banding party led by Frank Gress, who has extensively studied the only breeding colony of this species on the West Coast since its DDT-related decline in the 1970's.

PAGE 53: The coastal succulent *Carpobrotus chilense* forms dense patches on seacliffs, where it survives due to its ability to tolerate salt spray and make do with little fresh water.

The impeccable condition of the ranch buildings in the central valley of Santa Cruz Island reflects the concern of the owner, Dr. Carey Stanton, for conservation of the island's history and habitats.

PAGE 54: The tagging of elephant seals, such as this weaner handled by Brent Stewart and Chuck Oliver, has enabled scientists to accumulate data on the life history of individuals and of the species as a whole. One tagged young male, seen on Año Nuevo Island in the morning, was observed later the same day by other researchers on Farallon Island, sixty miles to the north.

FERTILE ROCKS: Año Nuevo and the Farallons

PAGE 56: In early autumn Año Nuevo Island is an important way station for California sea lions (*Zalophus californianus*) dispersing north from rookeries in the Channel Islands. At all times of the year it is the most important haul-out for pinnipeds utilizing the rich fishing grounds of Monterey Bay, which lacks other islands.

PAGE 61: Since the Coast Guard's withdrawal from Año Nuevo Island, sea lions have taken up residence in the lighthouse-keeper's house. Some make it to the second floor by way of the stairs; one animal died in the abandoned bathtub.

Año Nuevo Island is easily spotted from U.S. Highway 1, but powerful binoculars are needed to show mainland observers how densely packed with marine mammals and birds this tiny island is.

PAGE 62: An unknown but significant number of seals and sea lions perish after getting trapped in fishing nets, pack strings, and other manmade flotsam.

PAGE 63: The only vegetation on Southeast Farallon Island is quickly pulled out in early spring by cormorants seeking nesting material. For most of the year the island's surface is barren rocks, inspiring one fisherman to call the place "loneliness covered with bird shit."

PAGE 65: Año Nuevo barely qualifies as an island, yet the narrow channel that separates it from the mainland is enough security for sea lions and seabirds. These creatures are wary of mainland shores, where they are vulnerable to predation and harassment.

PAGE 67: Elephant seal pups are weaned at the age of four weeks. Once they have lost their mother's protection, they form pods at the periphery of the rookery to avoid being trampled by marauding bulls or bitten by nervous cows. The weaners in this photograph have already shed the black fur of babyhood but will not enter the water for another six weeks.

PAGE 68: The Farallons' lack of sheltered beaches necessitates a cumbersome landing procedure involving a crane and a basket, and even this is only possible in relatively calm weather.

PAGE 69: A former Coast Guard station on Southeast Farallon Island now houses a small crew of field biologists from the Point Reyes Bird Observatory. Personnel are relieved every six weeks, if all goes well; during the El Niño winter storms of 1982 no boat was able to land on the island for almost three months.

Only a few dozen tufted puffins (*Fratercula cirrhata*) nest on Southeast Farallon Island, which is at the southern end of their range. By comparison, a small island just north of Vancouver Island hosts over 50,000 pairs each summer.

PAGES 70 and 74: These engravings by E. A. Abbey accompanied an article about the Farallon Islands in Harper's new *Monthly Magazine* of April 1874.

PAGE 71: The Middle Farallons are off-limits to anyone not equipped with wings or flippers; even researchers observe them only from a distance.

PAGE 72: Wildlife biologist Larry Spear knows western gulls (*Larus occidentalis*) perhaps better than anyone else due to his extensive studies on the Farallons and elsewhere. Having traced the winter movements of gulls up and down the West Coast, he can point to individual birds breeding on the Farallons and tell you whether they spend the winter in Santa Barbara or around a dump in Newport, Oregon. He sometimes receives mail addressed to Dr. Larus Spear.

PAGE 73: Common murres (*Uria aalge*), like many other seabirds, return to the same mate and nest site year after year. The PRBO biologists who determined this have also been able to recognize individual birds in the dense colony from one season to the next by slight irregularities in their plumage.

PAGE 75: Black brant geese (*Branta bernicla*) commute twice a year between wintering areas in Baja's coastal lagoons and breeding grounds in Alaska and Siberia. Their spring migration along the West Coast coincides with the advent of strong northwest winds. This bird was exhausted from beating against a twenty-knot wind and slept for hours before joining another flock passing by Año Nuevo Island on its way north.

PAGE 76: According to William Dawson, an early chronicler of birdlife in California, a western gull asks itself only two questions in life. The first: "Am I hungry?" The answer is always "Yes." The second: "Is that edible?" The answer: "I don't know, but I'll try." One result of such indiscriminate appetite is this collection of not-so-edible objects regurgitated by parents and young at their nests. Rejected items include transit-fare tickets, restaurant menus, and fishing lures.

GEM OF THE SAN JUANS: Orcas Island

PAGE 78: The view from Mount Constitution westward includes portions of the San Juan and Gulf Islands as well as parts of Vancouver Island.

PAGE 83: Meadow in early fall, Orcas Island.

PAGE 84: Commercial fishing boats are a minority among the 15,000 or more pleasure boats that tie up at San Juan Island's Friday Harbor every year.

PAGE 85: This map, drawn in 1791 by Juan Carrasco for Captain Alexandro Malaespina of the Royal Spanish Armada, is from a period when explorers sought a northwest passage linking the Pacific with the Atlantic. Some believed the Strait of Juan de Fuca to be the entrance to that fabled shortcut. *Courtesy Bancroft Library.*

PAGE 87:   Throughout the San Juan Islands life is rather pastoral, but of all the islands served by the State Ferry, the pace seems slowest on Lopez, called "Slowpez" by some. The biggest employers on the island are the high school and supermarket.

PAGES 88 and 89:   In 1859 war between Britain and the United States almost broke out over a pig on San Juan Island. An American settler, Lyman Cutlar, shot a hog belonging to the Hudson's Bay Company because it uprooted his potatoes. When Canadian-British authorities, who claimed possession of the island at the time, tried to arrest him, protests from American settlers brought a U.S. infantry unit to the island. British troops responded in kind, and for the following twelve years both countries maintained a military presence on this outpost in the Northwest. In 1874 Kaiser Wilhelm I, designated as arbitrator, ruled that San Juan Island should belong to the United States, and the British withdrew. The photograph on page 88 shows the British camp, that on page 89 shows the American camp. *Courtesy Provincial Archives of British Columbia.*

PAGE 91:   Hazy morning view from the ferry off San Juan Island.

PAGE 93:   Dawn over tidelands with marshgrass near Mud Bay, Orcas Island.

Harbor seals (*Phoca vitulina*) are common along the West Coast from Baja's desert shores all the way up to the icebergs of Alaska's Glacier Bay, yet they're little known. Wary and elusive, they slide into the water from their haul-outs on intertidal reefs as soon as they sense attention focused on them.

PAGE 95:   Douglas firs (*Pseudotsuga menziesii*) are the giants of the Pacific Northwest, reaching a height and girth exceeded only by California's sequoias. Few virgin stands, however, have been spared from the logger's axe.

John Muir's favorite bird, the water ouzel (*Cinclus mexicanus*), earns its other name, dipper, for its habit of incessant bobbing while perched alongside fast-flowing streams. It often pursues its insect prey underwater.

PAGE 96:   Industrialist John McMillan, who ran a company town in Roche Harbor, built this shrine to himself and his family on San Juan Island. The limestone table symbolizes the table around which his family would gather in the hereafter. Each chair holds the ashes of one family member. The broken column of the mausoleum signifies, according to a tourist brochure, "the unfinished state of man's work when the string of life is broken."

PAGE 97:   Drooping cedar boughs, Moran State Park, Orcas Island.

WHALES AND EAGLES: Vancouver Island

PAGE 100:   Magnificently strong and streamlined killer whales (*Orcinus orca*) are capable of overcoming even a blue whale, the largest of all animals—not unlike a pack of wolves bringing down a moose. Most of the orcas that frequent Johnstone Strait, however, seem to be content with catching salmon.

PAGE 105:   Even though tourist billboards cheerfully market parts of coastal British Columbia as "the sunshine coast," the name "rain coast" is a more apt description.

PAGE 106:   Telegraph Cove, a hamlet on the northeast coast of Vancouver Island, is owned and managed by longtime resident Fred Westell.

PAGE 107:   The sunflower star (*Picnopodia helianthoides*), seen here in a tidepool, may descend to 435 meters below sea level to overwhelm prey—fishes, crabs, and snails—with its 15,000 sucker feet. Bivalves are sometimes eaten whole and digested internally. This largest of all Pacific Coast seastars, ranging from Alaska to San Diego, has arms up to two feet long; it may nevertheless fall victim to another giant, the Alaskan king crab.

PAGE 109:   The thin, wavering scream of the bald eagle (*Haliaeetus leucocephalus*) can be heard all along the British Columbia coast. Not yet threatened here by the habitat loss and pesticides that have nearly wiped out the species south of the Canadian border, it still numbers in the thousands.

Opportunistic feeders, they will take any prey they can get, dead or alive, and often gather in groups at places where food is abundant. In late summer many fly upriver to feed on spawned-out salmon.

PAGE 110: The village of Gwayasdums, on Gilford Island, as it appeared in 1900, with plank houses and decorated facades. Today's villagers have adopted Anglo-style cabins and enjoy modern conveniences such as electricity at their remote settlement near Kincome Inlet. *Courtesy British Columbia Provincial Museum.*

PAGE 111: According to a legend of the Kwicksutaineuk band of Gwayasdums on Gilford Island, all the animals were once gathered for a dance inside a cave called Nawalagwatsi ("receptacle of magic"). A young woman sneaked up to observe them, and the animals, sensing her presence, sent Mouse outside to look around. The woman talked Mouse into reporting there was no intruder, and the animals resumed dancing, but again felt her presence. Three times Mouse was sent outside and three times he came back saying there was nobody. The fourth time all the animals went outside and found the woman. Embarrassed, they took her inside the cave and taught her the dance she had just witnessed, to take back to her own people. In Gwayasdums the Dance of the Animal Kingdom, which features Mouse, Bear, Squirrel, and more than a dozen other characters, is still performed during feasts in the village's longhouse, which is named after the cave. In the photograph, masks carved by Sam Johnson representing Sea Otter, Deer, Wolf, Owl, and Kingfisher are set at the entrance of Nawalagwatsi.

PAGE 112: Dressed in bearskin and holding his sealskin floats, a West Coast whaler of the Nuu-chach-nulth tribe poses for photographer Edward Curtis. Preparations for the tremendous task of taking a whale during this period included ritual bathing for four moons and enactment of the movements of wounded whales. *Courtesy British Columbia Provincial Museum.*

PAGE 113: *Ursus americanus* can weigh, according to photographer Tim Fitzharris, "as much as two or three refrigerators," but supports its massive bulk on a humble diet of berries and small rodents. On northern Vancouver Island black bears are a common sight around garbage dumps.

PAGE 115: In the summer of 1984 Kwakiutl chiefs gathered in the village of Hee-Ghums, on Watson Island, for the raising of a totem pole carved by Richard Hunt in honor of chief Fred Williams, who died a few years earlier. The Kwakiutl were forced to go underground with their rituals for several decades early in this century, when white authorities, intent on suppressing the native culture, outlawed the potlatch festival. This ban has never been repealed formally, but in the last two decades a revival of interest in native culture has taken place. The new Kwakiutl art produced for potlatches and other ceremonies rivals the old pieces that are now in museums all over the world.

Detail of a totem pole at a Nimpkish burial ground on Malcolm Island, executed in the distinctive Kwakiutl fashion.

PAGE 117: This bald eagle was killed by an illegal gunshot.

PAGE 118: Loggers pose with a giant Douglas fir in a British Columbia coastal forest, 1924. *Courtesy Provincial Archives of British Columbia.*

PAGE 119: Whale-watchers photographing a pod of orcas passing through Johnstone Strait.

PAGE 121: A placid summer evening near Bamfield, Vancouver Island.

PAGE 122: This engraving was made by an artist with Captain Cook's 1778 expedition. *Courtesy Bancroft Library.*

EPILOGUE: The View Ahead

PAGE 124: The view from Echachis Island over Clayoquot Sound looking towards Meares Island. The latter is currently the subject of a major logging controversy between MacMillan-Bloedel and an alliance of white and Indian residents.

PAGE 127: Sea otters (*Enhydra lutris*), nearly extirpated by the end of the last century through hunting, have made a comeback along much of the West Coast since the advent of strong conservation measures. Reintroduced to the west coast of Vancouver Island in the early 1970's, they have tripled in number to more than 300 since then.

PAGE 129: The totem pole depicts a character in the cosmology of the Tlingit people, Fog Woman, who ensures the annual return of the salmon upon which natives on the Northwest coast depended. The spawning runs are perceived as an act of grace on the part of salmon, which return to feed the people. The first salmon caught every year is to be treated with great respect, and its bones are to be returned to the river to assure future runs.

In the world view of the timber companies that now control much of the land in coastal British Columbia, there is not much space for Fog Woman, or salmon, for that matter. Old growth trees are described as "decadent timber," and a climax rainforest is called "an area of negative growth." Company billboards erected next to large-scale clearcuts promise reforestation, but few salmon return to streams clogged with silt from eroding hillsides. And few trees now growing in carefully managed production forests will ever reach the girth necessary to become a totem pole celebrating Fog Woman.

PAGES 130 and 131: Humpback whales (*Megaptera novaeangliae*) are widely distributed in all the world's oceans and, like some other creatures depicted in this book, range throughout North America's west coast, from central Baja north to the Chukchi Sea. An estimated 15,000 humpbacks existed in the North Pacific prior to the commercial-whaling era; though the species is now protected, fewer than 1,000 may survive.

PAGE 132: A bald eagle appears to be the lone inhabitant of this islet in Queen Charlotte Strait, at the northern end of Vancouver Island.

Selected Bibliography

Ascensíon, Father Antonio De La. "Account of the Voyage of Sebastián Vizcaíno." Translated by Henry R. Wagner. *California Historical Society Quarterly*, vol. VII, no. 4 (1928).

California State Water Resources Control Board. *Farallon Island*. Water Quality Monitoring Report no. 79-13, May 1979.

Cook, Captain James. *Voyages of Discovery*. Edited by John Barrow. 1901. Reprint. New York: E.P. Dutton, Everyman's Library, 1961.

Costanso, Miguel. *Portola Expedition of 1769–1770*. Berkeley: University of California Press, 1911.

DeVoto, Bernard. *The Course of Empire*. Boston: Houghton Mifflin Co., 1952.

Drake, Sir Francis. *The World Encompassed*. London: Hakluyt Society, 1854. Reprint. Argonaut Press, 1926.

Gleason, Duncan. *The Islands and Ports of California*. New York: Devin-Adair Co., 1958.

Gordon, Burton L. *Monterey Bay Area: Natural History and Cultural Imprints*. Pacific Grove, Calif.: Boxwood Press, 1974.

Hoover, Mildred B. *The Farallon Islands*. Stanford: Stanford University Press, 1932.

Kelley, Don Greame. *Edge of a Continent*. Palo Alto: American West, 1971.

Langsdorff, G. D. von. *Narrative of the Rezanof Voyage*. San Francisco: T. C. Russel, 1927.

Leatherwood, Stephen, and Reeves, Randall. *The Sierra Club Handbook of Whales and Dolphins*. San Francisco: Sierra Club Books, 1983.

LeBoeuf, Burney J., and Kaza, Stephanie. *The Natural History of Año Nuevo*. Pacific Grove, Calif.: Boxwood Press, 1981.

Meares, John. *Voyages Made in the Years 1788 and 1789 from China to the N.W. Coast of America*. 1790. Reprint. New York: DaCapo Press, 1967.

Pethick, Derek. *First Approaches to the Northwest Coast*. Vancouver: Douglas & McIntyre Ltd. 1976.

Power, Dennis M., ed. *The California Islands: Proceedings of a Multidisciplinary Symposium*. Santa Barbara, Calif.: Santa Barbara Museum of Natural History, 1980.

Scammon, Charles M. *The Marine Mammals of the Northwestern Coast of North America; Described and Illustrated, Together with an Account of the American Whale-fishery*. 1874. Reprint. New York: Dover Publications, 1968.

Scott, Peter, and Wayburn, Cynthia. *In the Ocean Wind*. Felton, Calif.: Glenwood Publishers, 1974.

Steinbeck, John. *The Log From the Sea of Cortez*. New York: Viking Press, 1951.

Thomas, Bill. *The Island*. New York: W. W. Norton, 1980.

U.S. Department of the Interior. *Channel Islands: Environmental Assessment, Natural and Cultural Resources Management Plan*. Washington, D.C.: National Park Service, 1980.

Vancouver, George. *A Voyage of Discovery to the North Pacific Ocean and Round the World*. 3 Vols. London: C.J. & J. Robinson, 1798.

INDEX

Italicized cites are to photographs and illustrations